For Reference

r608

C

Not to be taken from this roc

The Book of American Trade Marks, Volume 4

TradeMarks/4

The Annual of Trade Mark Design T.M.

David E. Carter

ART DIRECTION *BOOK* COMPANY

19 West 44th Street   New York, New York 10036

First Printing, March 1976
Second Printing 1977

No design in this book may be copied without
the permission of the owner of the mark.

ART DIRECTION BOOK COMPANY
19 West 44th Street
New York, New York 10036
212/986-4930

Library of Congress Catalog Card Number: 72-76493
International Standard Book Number: 0-910158-30-4
ISBN for Standing Orders for this series: 0-910158-38-X

How to submit marks for future volumes.

The Book of American Trade Marks is an annual publication, showing good examples of contemporary trade mark design.

Designers are invited to submit marks for possible inclusion in future volumes. Work submitted should adhere to the following guidelines:

(1) if at all possible, send the marks in the *actual size* they are to be reproduced in the book. This will permit your print to be used directly on the paste-up, and will assure that your mark reproduces well in the book.

(2) do *not* mount the work.

(3) include the name of the client, and the way you wish to be identified in the credit line. Include your address for the index.

(4) send a letter giving permission for the marks to be included in the book.

Due to the large number of marks received, it is impossible for receipt of your work to be acknowledged.

All material should be sent to David E. Carter, Post Office Box 591, Ashland, Kentucky 41101.

This book is dedicated to E. D. Mittendorf, who as Editor of *The Russell Times,* served a small community as a journalist and as a humanitarian.

3029

3033

3030

3034

3031

3035

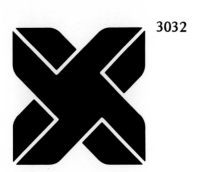

3032

3036

3037

3038

3039

3029 Bradford-Pittman Travel
Designer: James L. Potocki

3030 Woodland Hills
Designer: James L. Potocki

3031 IT Cosmetics
Designer: James L. Potocki

3032 Compass Computer Services
Designer: Bruce Cockerill;
James Potocki & Associates

3033 Keystone Mortgage Co.
Designer: James L. Potocki

3034 The McDonald Company
Designer: Paul Holmquist;
James Potocki & Associates

3035 Huttas and Potocki
Designer: Paul Holmquist;
James Potocki & Associates

3036 Community Cablevision Company
Designer: James Potocki/Roy Ritola

3037 Unicorn Systems Company
Designer: James Potocki

3038 Carlsberg Financial
Designer: James Potocki

3039 Liquidity Fund Inc.
Designer: James Potocki;
Huerta Design Associates

3040

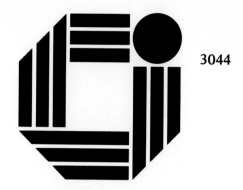

3044

Kangaroo

3041

CONCEPT

3042

SDParkerCompany

3043

NORTHWEST PIPELINE CORPORATION

3045

3046

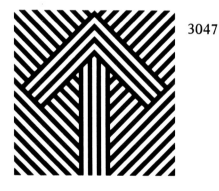

3047

3040 Management Accounting Package/Unicorn
Designer: James Potocki;
James Potocki & Associates

3041 Kangaroo Campers
Designer: James Potocki;
James Potocki & Associates

3042 Concept
Designer: James Potocki;
James Potocki & Associates

3043 S.D. Parker Co.
Designer: James Potocki;
James Potocki & Associates

3044 National Credit Information Service
Designer: James Potocki;
Huerta Design Associates

3045 Northwest Pipeline Corporation
Designer: Reeves, Dyke and Co.

3046 Seaton Industries
Designer: E.W. Baker, Inc.

3047 Houston/Ritz/Cohen/Jagoda
Designer: Wayne Houston

3048 The LTV Corporation
Designer: Walter Landor Associates

THE LTV CORPORATION

3048

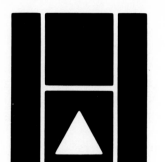

3049

3053

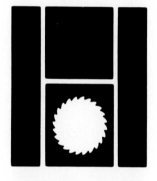

3050

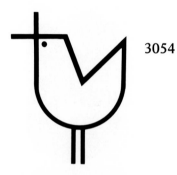

3054

3051

3055

3052

ALLIS-CHALMERS

3056

3057

3058

Hethwood

3059

3060

3049 Hill Acme Company
      Designer: Evan Kiousis

3050 Loma Machine & Mfg. Co.
      Designer: Evan Kiousis

3051 Sherwood Selpac Co.
      Designer: Evan Kiousis

3052 Allis-Chalmers
      Designer: Gerald Stahl

3053 Harris Trust and Savings Bank
      Designer: Schecter and Luth

3054 Terrace View Apartments
      Designer: Harvey C. Dellinger

3055 Mission Hill
      Designer: Harvey C. Dellinger

3056 Haymarket Square Townhouses
      Designer: Harvey C. Dellinger

3057 Foxridge Apartments
      Designer: Harvey C. Dellinger

3058 Hethwood
      Designer: Harvey C. Dellinger

3059 Bruce Machinery
      Designer: Harvey C. Dellinger

3060 Broadacres Shopping Center
      Designer: Harvey C. Dellinger

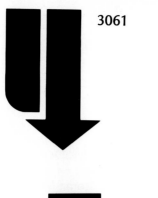
3061

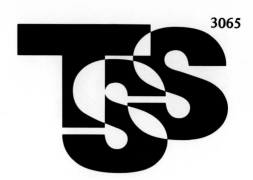
3065

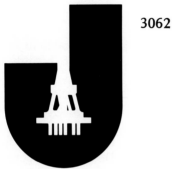
3062

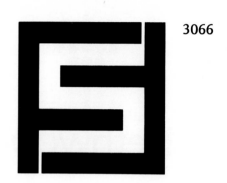
3066

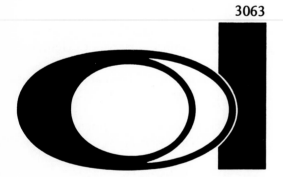
3063

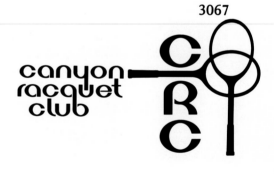
3067

canyon racquet club

3064

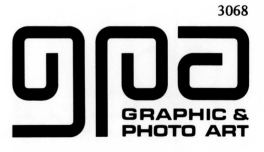
3068

GRAPHIC &
PHOTO ART

Hershey Foods 3069

Hexon 3070

Allied Chemical 3071

3072 TOLEDO EDISON

3061 Underground Vaults & Storage, Inc.
Designer: Ronald Muhlenbruch;
Lane & Leslie

3062 Johnson Drill Head Co.
Designer: Ronald Muhlenbruch;
Lane & Leslie

3063 Doerr Metal Products
Designer: Lane & Leslie

3064 The Genealogical Institute
Designer: Peter J. Rabe;
Graphic & Photo Art

3065 Transportation Safety Systems
Designer: Peter J. Rabe;
Graphic & Photo Art

3066 For-Shor Company
Designer: Peter J. Rabe;
Graphic & Photo Art

3067 Canyon Racquet Club
Designer: Peter J. Rabe;
Graphic & Photo Art

3068 Graphic & Photo Art
Designer: Peter J. Rabe;
Graphic & Photo Art

3069 Hershey Foods
Hershey, Pennsylvania

3070 Hexon
Designer: Bradford-La Riviera

3071 Allied Chemical Corporation
Designer: Lubliner/Saltz, Inc.

3072 Toledo Edison
Toledo, Ohio

 3073

 3077

 3074

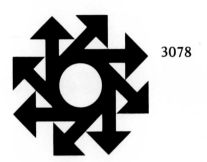 3078

3075

3079

3076

3080

The Benchmark

3081

Wedgewood

3082

THE WOODLANDS

3083

COUNTRY PLACE

3084

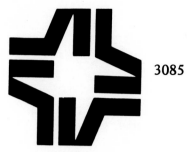 3085

 3089

 3086

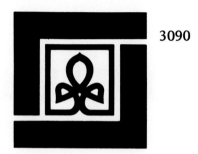 3090

 3087

 3091

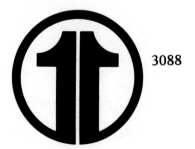 3088

 3092

 3093

 3094

 3095

 3096

3085 Mark IV Properties, Inc.
Designer: Wyatt L. Phillips

3086 Post Properties, Inc.
Designer: Wyatt L. Phillips

3087 Bothwell, Jenkins, Slay & Assoc., Architects
Designer: Wyatt L. Phillips

3088 The First National Bank of Tucker
Designer: Phillips & Associates

3089 Cox Hotel Management
Designer: Wyatt L. Phillips

3090 Lafayette Square Apartments
Designer: Wyatt L. Phillips

3091 Guthrie Realty Company
Designer: Phillips & Associates, Inc.

3092 The Marketing Advisory Group
Designer: Wyatt L. Phillips;
The Marketing Advisory Group

3093 North National Properties
Designer: Wyatt L. Phillips

3094 Winchester Office Park
Designer: Phillips & Associates, Inc.

3095 Motor Inn Management
Designer: Wyatt L. Phillips

3096 Loch Highland Subdivision
Designer: Wyatt L. Phillips

3097

3101

3098

3102

3099

3103

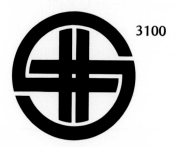
3100

3104

Aspen Land Company

3105

3106

3107

SHIMANO

3108

3097 The Lakes Apartments
Designer: Phillips & Associates, Inc.

3098 Greenbriar Acres Subdivision
Designer: Phillips & Associates, Inc.

3099 Interchange Village
Designer: Wyatt L. Phillips

3100 Four Seasons Racquet Club
Designer: Wyatt L. Phillips

3101 Northlake Square Office Park
Designer: Wyatt L. Phillips;
The Marketing Advisory Group

3102 Villas West Mobile Home Park
Designer: Wyatt L. Phillips

3103 Laurelwood Apartments
Designer: Wyatt L. Phillips

3104 Lehndorff Management (USA) Ltd.
Designer: Wyatt L. Phillips

3105 Aspen Land Company
Designer: Wyatt L. Phillips

3106 Spartek Inc.
Designer: Jay H. Maish Co.

3107 Kaufman and Broad Inc.
Los Angeles

3108 Shimano Sales Corporation
Designer: Yoshi Oda

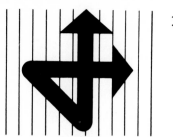 3109

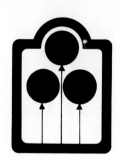 3113

 3110

3114

SIGNASEAL

 3111

3115

 3112

3116

3117

3118

3119

3120

3109 Geoffrey Ladhams Associates
Designer: Monte J. Curry;
Monte J. Curry Marketing

3110 Plasmold, Inc.
Designer: Monte J. Curry

3111 Providence Properties, Inc.
Designer: Monte J. Curry

3112 Decorative Components Division,
Polysar Plastics, Inc.
Designer: Elaine M. Lyerly;
Monte J. Curry Marketing

3113 River Hills Plantation (special celebration)
Designer: Elaine M. Lyerly;
Monte J. Curry Marketing

3114 Signseal
Designer: Elaine M. Lyerly;
Monte J. Curry Marketing

3115 Repro/Graphics
Designer: Elaine M. Lyerly;
Monte J. Curry Marketing

3116 Media-Concepts, Inc.
Designer: Monte J. Curry

3117 Apartment Locator Service
Designer: Monte J. Curry

3118 The Cove Condominium
Designer: Elaine M. Lyerly
Monte J. Curry Marketing

3119 Street Development Company
Designer: Monte J. Curry

3120 D.C. Turner Construction Co.
Designer: Monte J. Curry

 3121

 3125

 3122

 3126

 3123

 3127

 3124

 3128

3129

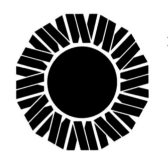

3130

3131

3132

3121 Modern Management, Inc.
Designer: Elaine M. Lyerly;
Monte J. Curry Marketing

3122 The Lodge
Designer: Elaine M. Lyerly;
Monte J. Curry Marketing

3123 Pat Wagner Communications
Designer: Monte J. Curry

3124 Mimosa Hills Golf Club
Designer: Elaine M. Lyerly;
Monte J. Curry Marketing

3125 Providence Square Racquet Club
Designer: Monte J. Curry

3126 Gordon Gutke Advertising Art
Designer: Gordon Gutke Advertising Art

3127 Travel Desk (travel agency)
Designer: Gordon Gutke Advertising Art

3128 Century Incentives
Designer: Gordon Gutke Advertising Art

3129 Fabricators Inc.
Designer: Gordon Gutke Advertising Art

3130 Washington County (proposed)
Designer: Gordon Gutke Advertising Art

3131 J. Plush Brush (beauty parlor)
Designer: Gordon Gutke Advertising Art

3132 Insta-Just (hydraulic chair)
Designer: Gordon Gutke Advertising Art

 3133

 3137

 3134

 3138

 3135

 3139

 3136

 3140

3141

3142

3143

3144

3133 Krengel Machine Company, Inc.
Designer: Gordon Gutke Advertising Art

3134 C and L Business Systems
Designer: Gordon Gutke Advertising Art

3135 Brown Equipment Co.
Designer: Gordon Gutke Advertising Art

3136 Ute Research Laboratories
Designer: Gordon Gutke Advertising Art

3137 Gateway Finance Company
Designer: Gordon Gutke Advertising Art

3138 Concept Industries Corporation
Designer: Gordon Gutke Advertising Art

3139 Trevarrow, Inc.
Designer: Al Weston

3140 Miramos
Designer: Rolf H. Paul Graphics

3141 West Nebraska General Hospital
Designer: Rolf H. Paul Graphics

3142 Black Hawk Enterprises
Designer: Rolf H. Paul Graphics

3143 The Market Place
Designer: Rolf H. Paul Graphics

3144 American Lightbulb Supply Co.
Designer: Rolf H. Paul Graphics

 3145

 3149

 3146

 3150

 3147

 3151

 3148

 3152

 3153

 3154

 3155

3156

3145 Bulldog Enterprises
Designer: Rolf H. Paul Graphics

3146 Wells Inc.
Designer: Rolf H. Paul Graphics

3147 Monticore
Designer: Rolf H. Paul Graphics

3148 Transportation Adv. Associates
Designer: Mike Miller; Graphic Art Services

3149 Roy Clark
Designer: Mike Miller; Graphic Art Services

3150 Alpine Pest Control
Designer: Mike Miller; Graphic Art Services

3151 Mom Productions
Designer: Mike Miller; Graphic Art Services

3152 Cabaret Productions
Designer: Mike Miller; Graphic Art Services

3153 Joanne Halsey
Designer: John Dykema; Graphic Art Services

3154 Institute of Pastoral Counseling
Designer: Herb Hansen; Graphic Art Services

3155 Royal Foods
Designer: Mike Miller; Graphic Arts Services

3156 Lindy's — Flamingo Hotel
Designer: Mike Miller; Graphic Art Services

 3157

 3161

 3158

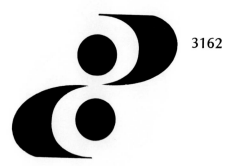 3162

 3159

 3163

3160

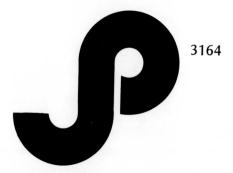 3164

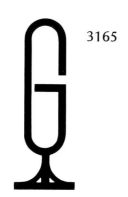

3165

3166

3167

3157 JCS Bench Company
Designer: Mike Miller; Graphic Art Services

3158 Five Companies Inc.
Designer: Mike Miller; Graphic Art Services

3159 Landmark Hotel
Designer: Mike Miller; Graphic Art Services

3160 Cambridge Racquet Club
Designer: Mike Miller; Graphic Art Services

3161 Family Doctors of Nevada
Designer: Mike Miller; Graphic Art Services

3162 KLAS-TV 8
Designer: Mike Miller; Graphic Art Services

3163 Jim Halsey Company
Designer: Mike Miller; Graphic Art Services

3164 Joe Peterson Interiors
Designer: Mike Miller; Graphic Art Services

3165 Gentry Sound
Designer: Herb Hansen; Graphic Art Services

3166 B & G International
Designer: Mike Miller; Graphic Art Services

3167 Pagama Productions
Designer: Mike Miller; Graphic Art Services

3168 Flamingo Hotel
Designer: Mike Miller; Graphic Art Services

3168

 3169

 3173

 3170

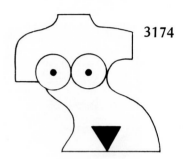 3174

 3171

 3174

 3172

 3176

 3177

 3178

 3179

 3180

3169 Home Savings and Loan Association
Designer: Lawrence E. Pelini

3170 Kewanee National Bank
Designer: Lawrence E. Pelini

3171 Lawrence E. Pelini Studio Ltd.
Designer: Lawrence E. Pelini

3172 Association for Modern Banking in Illinois
Designer: Lawrence E. Pelini

3173 Heart of Illinois Beef Association
Designer: Lawrence E. Pelini

3174 Brenda/Artists Model
Designer: Lawrence E. Pelini

3175 Westchester Library System
White Plains, New York

3176 First Empire Bank — New York
Designer: Paul Sandhaus Associates

3177 O'Connor Realty
Designer: Funk Advertising Company

3178 Taylor Building Products
Designer: Kevin Tolman; Artra Associates

3179 Brand Names Foundation, Inc.
Designer: Paul Hansbursin

3180 Mountain House
Oregon Freeze Dry Foods, Inc.
Albany, Oregon

3181

3182

3183

3184

3185

3186

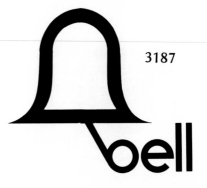

3187

3188

3189

3190

3191

3192

INCORPORATED

3181 Tempo Leasing Corp.
Designer: Douglas C. Granger;
Leslie Advertising

3182 Recordplate Company, Inc.
Designer: James M. Walker

3183 American Pioneer Center
Designer: Alan Leitstein

3184 "The Links" Golf Country Club
Designer: Alan Leitstein

3185 Alan Stuart Leitstein
Designer: Alan Leitstein

3186 Florida Living Center
Designer: Alan Leitstein

3187 Bell Mortgage Corporation
Designer: Alan Leitstein

3188 C.E. Industries Inc.
Designer: Alan Leitstein

3189 PSI Industries
Designer: William W. Chapman;
CPS Communications

3190 Plico Products
Designer: William W. Chapman;
CPS Communications

3191 Texas Plasticote Inc.
Designer: William W. Chapman/
Robert Giaimo; CPS
Communications

3192 NRG Incorporated
Designer: Kidder Axelson
& Associates, Inc.

 3193

 3197

 3194

 3198

The Communications Board 3195

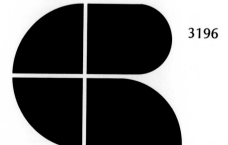 3196

3199

3200

3201

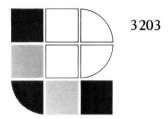

3202

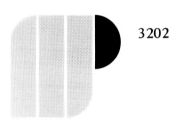

3203

3204

 3205

 3209

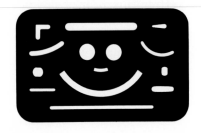 3206

 3210

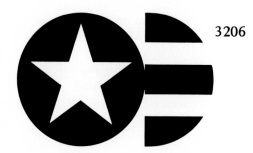 3207

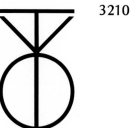 3211

 3208

 3212

 3213

Dan River® 3214

3215

3216

3205 Western Bass Anglers Association
Designer: Mike Quon

3206 Outagamie Democtars
Designer: Pat Taylor

3207 Kimberly-Clark Corp. (Erasable Bond)
Designer: Pat Taylor

3208 Gerry Kanode
Designer: Pat Taylor

3209 Urban Land Perspectives Inc.
Designer: Pat Taylor

3210 TYO Publishing Co.
Designer: Pat Taylor

3211 Dana Research Inc.
Designer: Pat Taylor

3212 Combined Communications Corporation
Designer: Barry Wickliffe

3212 The Sherwin-Williams Company
Designer: F. Eugene Smith Associates

3214 Dan River Inc.
Designer: Sandgren & Murtha, Inc.

3215 Xeroil Corporation
Designer: Don A. Primi; Industrial Advertising
       Associates, Inc.

3216 Flightline
Designer: Milton Chun

3217

3218

3219

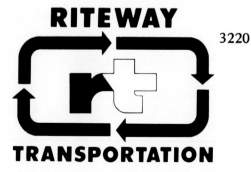
3220

3221

3222

3223

3224

3225

3226

3227

3217 Mique Quenzer Directions Inc.
Designer: Milton Chun

3218 Diversified Graphic Impressions
Designer: Frank A. Gutierrez

3219 Pro-Motions
Designer: Frank A. Gutierrez

3220 Riteway Transportation
Designer: Frank A. Gutierrez

3221 Alec Litho
Designer: Frank A. Gutierrez

3222 Cano Electric
Designer: Frank A. Gutierrez

3223 Z.A.C. Charro Association (Mexican Rodeo)
Designer: Frank A. Gutierrez

3224 Spanish-American Institute
Designer: Frank A. Gutierrez

3225 Pat McCormick Enterprises
Designer: Frank A. Gutierrez

3226 College of Agriculture and Life Sciences Fund
Designer: James K. Estes

3227 Bank of New Hampshire N.A.
Manchester, New Hampshire

3228 William Seifert
Designer: William Seifert

3228

William Seifert
graphic design photography
350 East 52nd street
apt. 12-K
New York New York 10022

3229

3233

3220

3234

3231

3235

3232

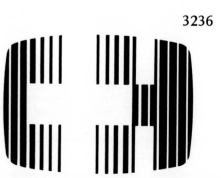

3236

3237

3238

3239

3240

3229 The Drake Office
      Designer: Melville M. Drake

3230 Pro-Mote, Inc.
      Designer: Melville M. Drake

3231 Republic Savings & Loan
      Designer: Melville M. Drake

3232 New Process Corporation
      Designer: Melville M. Drake

3233 Brookfield Hills
      Designer: Melville M. Drake

3234 Logan & Associates
      Designer: Melville M. Drake

3235 Wilson, Haas & Associates, Inc.
      Designer: Melville M. Drake

3236 Communications for Hospitals, Inc.
      Designer: Richard Morgado Designer

3237 Crotched Mountain
      Designer: Richard Morgado Designer

3238 Glen Terrace Nurseries
      Designer: Anita Soos

3239 Warsaw Agency
      Designer: Anita Soos

3240 Office Interiors, Inc.
      Designer: Anita Soos

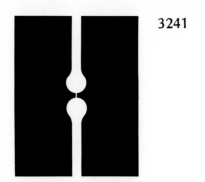

3241

3245

3242

3246

3243

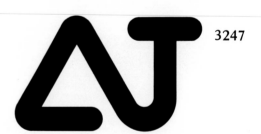

3247

3244

3248

3249

Career Directions

3250

3251

3252

3241 Heinsz Insurance Agency, Inc.
Designer: Anita Soos

3242 Edward J. Smith Assocs./Advertising
Designer: Anita Soos

3243 Carl Scholl Insurance
Designer: Anita Soos

3244 Potter Insurance Agency
Designer: Anita Soos

3245 Palm Beach Insurance Central, Inc.
Designer: Anita Soos

3246 Emery-Webb, Inc.
Designer: Anita Soos

3247 Arnold Jones Insurance Agency
Designer: Anita Soos

3248 Fulmer & Company
Designer: Anita Soos

3249 Aetna Life & Casualty
Designer: Anita Soos

3250 Larson, Raikko & Weaver, Inc.
Designer: Anita Soos

3251 Tubertini-Hillhouse Insurance Agency, Inc.
Designer: Anita Soos

3252 Nussear Insurance Agency, Inc.
Designer: Anita Soos

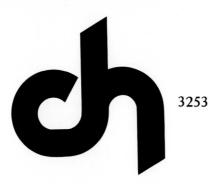 3253

 3257

 3254

 3258

 3255

 3259

 3256

 3260

 3261

 3262

 3263

3253 Crowell C. Hall
Designer: Anita Soos

3254 Small World Childrens Day School
Designer: Jess Gruel; Larson-Bateman, Inc.

3255 Quadrant Development Corp.
Designer: Jess Gruel; Larson-Bateman, Inc.

3256 Santa Barbara Photo Engravers
Designer: Jess Gruel; Larson-Bateman, Inc.

3257 Bank of Montecito
Designer: Jess Gruel; Larson-Bateman, Inc.

3258 Jolly Tiger Restaurants
Designer: Jess Gruel; Larson-Bateman, Inc.

3259 Oakcrest
Designer: Jess Gruel; Larson-Bateman, Inc.

3260 Tierra Cavo
Designer: Jess Gruel; Larson-Bateman, Inc.

3261 Michael Towbes Construction Co.
Designer: Jess Gruel; Larson-Bateman, Inc.

3262 Boulder Creek Golf & Country Club
Designer: Jess Gruel; Larson-Bateman, Inc.

3263 Calvary Presbyterian Church
Designer: Everett Forbes

3264 Vanguard Advertising, Inc.
Designer: Everett Forbes

 3264

 3265

 3269

 3266

 3270

 3267

 3271

3268

3272

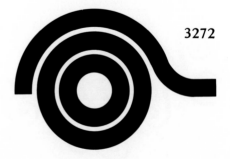

 3273

 3274

3265 Bayside Hospital
Designer: Everett Forbes

3266 The Colonies
Designer: Everett Forbes

3267 Dorey Electrical Contractors
Designer: Everett Forbes

3268 Yancey Brothers Co.
Designer: Robert C. Manning

3269 Arkansas Society of Communication Arts
Designer: Tom Henton

3270 Markham Inn Hotel
Designer: Tom Henton

3271 Capital Club
Designer: Tom Henton

 3275

3272 Roberts Brothers Tire Service
Designer: Tom Henton

3273 Varco-Pruden, Inc.
Designer: Tom Henton

3274 Faulkner-Watkins & Assocs.
Designer: Tom Henton

3275 Pacesetter Corporation
Designer: Tom Henton

 3276

3276 AFCO Metals, Inc.
Designer: Tom Henton

3277

3281

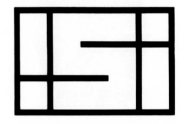

3278

3282

3279

3283

3280

3284

Citibank

3285

3286

3287

Scovill

3288

3277 Creative Leisure
Designer: Steven Jacobs Designs

3278 Ram Ridge Corporate Park
Designer: Robert A. Gale

3279 Chelsea Industries
Designer: Robert A. Gale

3280 Chimney Hill Corporation
Designer: Robert A. Gale

3281 Croydon, subsidiary of Uniroyal, Inc.
Designer: Robert A. Gale

3282 Innovative Sciences, Inc.
Designer: Robert A. Gale

3283 Gilded Coach Services Limosine Service
Designer: Robert A. Gale

3284 First National City Bank
Designer: Robert A. Gale

3285 The Clare Laughlin Travel Services, Inc.
Designer: Robert A. Gale

3286 First National City Bank
Designer: Robert A. Gale

3287 Salvation Discotheque
Designer: Robert A. Gale

3288 Scovill Manufacturing Company
Designer: Robert A. Gale

 3289

 3293

 3290

 3294

 3291

 3295

 3292

 3296

PUBLICITY/PUBLIC RELATIONS

3298

PALMBROOK
COUNTRY CLUB

3299

secluded*acres

3300

Chaparral Rancheros

3289 Rainbow Slump Block Co.
      Designer: Marie Martel

3290 Distinctive Designs
      Designer: Marie Martel

3291 Professional Corporation Portfolios
      Designer: Marie Martel

3292 National Speakers Association
      Designer: Marie Martel

3293 Estrella Ranch
      Designer: Marie Martel

3294 Marina City Club
      Designer: Marie Martel

3295 Aid to Zoo Horse Show
      Designer: Marie Martel

3296 Sickles Sales & Service
      Designer: Marie Martel

3297 Maxine Olmsted Publicity
      Designer: Marie Martel

3298 Palmbrook Country Club
      Designer: Marie Martel

3299 Secluded Acres
      Designer: Marie Martel

3300 Chaparral Rancheros
      Designer: Marie Martel

 3301

 3305

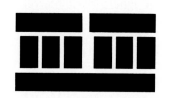 3302

 3306

 3303

 3307

 3304

 3308

3309

3310

3311

3312

 3313

 3317

 3314

Prudential Plaza

 3318

 3315

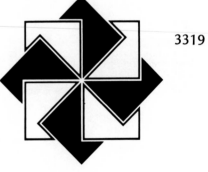 3319

 3316

 3320

L.C. Jacobson

3321

3322

3323

3324

 3325

 3329

 3326

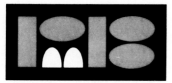

 3330

 3327

 3331

 3328

 3332

 3333

 3334

 3335

 3336

3325 Sunland Paper Company
Designer: Marie Martel

3326 Romar, Inc.
Designer: Marie Martel

3327 R.M. Bowlsby & Associates
Designer: Marie Martel

3328 Valley Beautiful Citizens Council, Inc.
Designer: Marie Martel

3329 Val Moritz
Designer: Marie Martel

3330 R.M. Wartes
Designer: Marie Martel

3331 Cara Nova, Inc.
Designer: Marie Martel

3332 Cash, Sullivan & Cross
Designer: Marie Martel

3333 Del Webb's Towne House
Designer: Marie Martel

3334 Plaza Liquors
Designer: Marie Martel

3335 Los Angeles Music & Art School
Designer: Frank A. Gutierrez

3336 Fair Lawn Industries, Inc.
Designer: David Leigh

3337

3341

3338

3342

3339

3343

3340

3344

 3345

 3346

 3347

 3348

3349

3353

3350

3354

3355

3351

ESMARK 3352

3356

3357

3358

3359

3349 Mariner's Resort Inn
        Designer: Everett Forbes

3350 Chewning, Hoggard, Adkins, Engineers
        Designer: Everett Forbes

3351 Lloyd Chester Associates
        Designer: Mike Quon

3352 Esmark, Inc.
        Designer: Anspach, Grossman Inc.

3353 University of Rochester, Student Activities
            Center
        Designer: Stephen Reynolds

3354 Enterprise Press
        Designer: Stephen Reynolds

3355 SMH-Art Council
        Designer: Stephen Reynolds

3356 Morgan Yacht Corporation
        Designer: Bradley Yeager;
            Bradley Yeager & Associates, Inc.

3357 Public Information, Inc.
        Designer: Joe Dill; Bradley Yeager & Associates

3358 Easton Realty
        Designer: Gary Brown;
            Bradley Yeager & Associates, Inc.

3359 Oak Lake Park
        Designer: Gary Brown;
            Bradley Yeager & Associates, Inc.

3360

MarinerVillage

3364

 JERGER & SONS, INC.

3361

Kuttler

3365

 75th anniversary we weren't born yesterday

3362

 IMPERIAL PALMS VILLAGE

3363

3366

 **Winding Creek**

3367

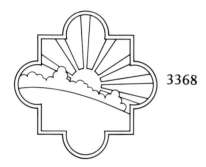

3368

3369

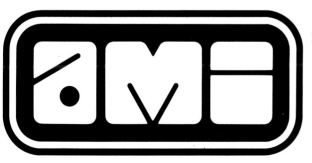

3370

3360 Mariner Village
Designer: Joe Dill; Bradley Yeager & Associates

3361 Carl Kuttler
Designer: Gary Brown
   Bradley Yeager & Associates, Inc.

3362 Imperial Palms Village
Designer: Joe Dill; Bradley Yeager & Associates

3363 Bruce Little Co., Plumbing
Designer: Joe Dill; Bradley Yeager & Associates

3364 Jerger & Sons, Inc.
Designer: Gary Brown;
   Bradley Yeager & Associates, Inc.

3365 Ellis First National Bank
Designer: Gary Brown;
   Bradley Yeager & Associates, Inc.

3366 Winding Creek
Designer: Gary Brown;
   Bradley Yeager & Associates, Inc.

3367 Rodgers & Associates
Designer: Marvin L. Joseph

3368 Serinada Country Estates
Designer: Joseph Advertising Design

3369 Dave Shanks
Designer: Marvin L. Joseph

3370 Austin Meters Inc.
Designer: Joseph Advertising Design

3371

 =PAL-CHEM INDUSTRIES, INC.

3375

3372

BABCOCK, CO.

3376

3373

3374

CRAFTS & CULTURE

3377

3378

3371 Pal-Chem Industries, Inc.
Designer: Joseph Advertising Design

3372 Babcock Co.
Designer: Marvin L. Joseph

3373 Knight, Walsh & Associates, Inc.
Designer: Kerry Walsh; Knight, Walsh & Assocs.

3374 Crafts & Culture
Designer: Knight, Walsh & Associates

3375 College of the Ozarks
Designer: Knight, Walsh & Associates

3376 Tonkawa High School, Class of 64 Reunion
Designer: Knight, Walsh & Associates

3379

3377 Peoples Gas Co.
Designer: Arnold La Bahn, Robert Sychowski

3378 R. K. P. Associates
Designer: Jonathan Pieslak

3379 Jonathan Pieslak
Designer: Jonathan Pieslak

3380 Rae Real Estate and Management Co.
Designer: Jonathan Pieslak

3380

rae real estate
and management
company

ROBERT ANTHONY
PRESENTATIONS
LECTURES / SEMINARS / BROADCASTING

3381

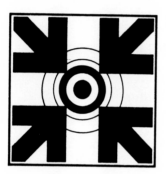

3382

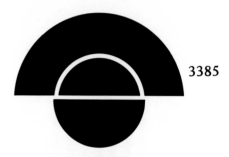

3385

3383

3386

3384

3387

3388

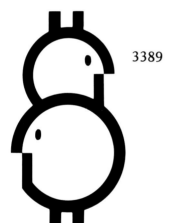

3389

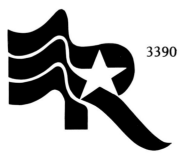

3390

3381 Robert Anthony Presentations
       Designer Michael Kowalczyk

3382 New England Site Locators
       Designer: Michael Kowalczyk

3383 Riccardo Caine Photography
       Designer: Michael Kowalczyk

3384 Edward A. Saunders
       Designer: Edward A. Saunders

3385 Halawa Grand Condominium
       Designer: Edward A. Saunders

3386 "Kekuaananui" Hawaii Big Sisters, Inc.
       Designer: Edward A. Saunders

3387 Hawaiian Mortgage Co., Inc.
       Designer: Edward A. Saunders

3388 Hawaiian Banana Company
       Designer: Edward A. Saunders

3389 Reliable Finance Inc.
       Designer: Ray Ainsworth

3390 Reliable Finance Inc.
       Designer: Ray Ainsworth

3391

3394

3392

3395

3393

WABE
FM90.1

3396

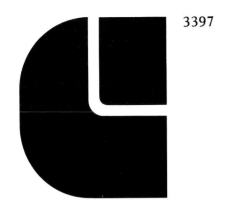

3397

3398

3399

3400

CHINESE AMERICAN INSTITUTE

WETV30

3401

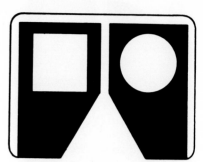

3404

3402

RI

3405

3403

BECA

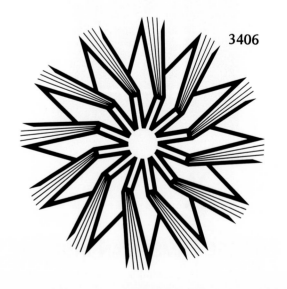

3406

3407

3408

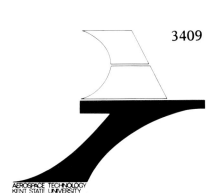

3409

3410

3401 Public Broadcasting Atlanta
      Designer: Steve Skaggs

3402 Tri-County Bank
      Designer: Steve Skaggs

3403 Business Equipment Center of Atlanta, Inc.
      Designer: Steve Skaggs

3404 Teacher's Guide, TV Channel 21
      Designer: Paul S. Weiser

3405 Paul S. Weiser
      Designer: Paul S. Weiser

3406 Manager's Planner, Xerox
      Designer: Paul S. Weiser

3407 WKSU-TV, Kent State University
      Designer: Paul S. Weiser

3408 New York State Road Racing Championship
      Designer: Paul S. Weiser

3409 Aerospace Technology, Kent State University
      Designer: Paul S. Weiser

3410 Modular Scientific Corporation
      Designer: Paul S. Weiser

3411

SUPERIOR
DESIGN CO., INC.

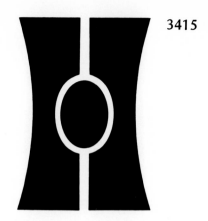

3415

3412

car
care
council

3416

3413

3414

GRAFIX

3417

3418

3419

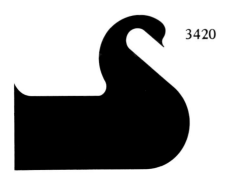

3420

3411 Superior Design, Inc.
Designer: Paul S. Weiser

3412 Car Care Council
Dearborn, Michigan

3413 Sugarcreek Concepts
Designer: Reginald K. Litten

3414 Reg Litten Grafix
Designer: Reginald K. Litten

3415 The Hewitt Soap Co., Inc.
Designer: Reginald K. Litten

3416 Bramkamp Printing Co., Inc.
Designer: Reginald K. Litten

3417 Perfection Tool & Mold Corporation
Designer: Reginald K. Litten

3418 Kickham Boiler and Engineering, Inc.
Designer: Mel Zimmerman

3419 The Graphic Statement
Designer: Michael Pacey/Supergraphics

3420 The Sleeping Bird (antique shop)
Designer: Michael Pacey/Supergraphics

3421

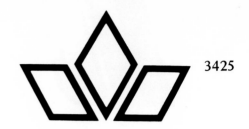

3425

3422

3426

3423

3427

3424

3428

3429

3430

3431

3432

THE JEFFERSON SQUARE

3421 YWCA
Designer: J. David Suggs

3422 Flexi Wall Corporation
Designer: J. David Suggs

3423 Project Haiti
Designer: J. David Suggs

3424 South Carolina Department of
Parks, Recreation and Tourism
Designer: J. David Suggs

3425 South Carolina Tricentennial Celebration
Designer: J. David Suggs

3426 Columbia Drug Response Celebration
Designer: J. David Suggs

3427 South Carolina Department of Mental Health
Designer: J. David Suggs

3428 Standard Corporation and the
Standard Warehouse Company
Designer: J. David Suggs

3429 South Carolina Department of Social Services
Designer: J. David Suggs

3430 South Carolina Baptist Campus Ministries
Designer: J. David Suggs

3431 Pentagon Corporation
Designer: J. David Suggs

3432 The Jefferson Square Theatre
Designer: J. David Suggs

 3433

 3437

 3438

 3434

 3435

 3439

 3436

 3440

 3441

 3442

 3443

 3444

3433 Greater Carolinas Corporation
      Designer: J. David Suggs

3434 Alston Wilkes Society
      Designer: J. David Suggs

3435 Fox Music House
      Designer: J. David Suggs

3436 Contact Help
      Designer: J. David Suggs

3437 Carolina Coliseum
      Designer: J. David Suggs

3438 Eve's Apple Incorporated
      Designer: J. David Suggs

3439 Columbia Bible College
      Designer: J. David Suggs

3440 First Federal Savings & Loan Association
      Designer: J. David Suggs

3441 Greater Myrtle Beach Chamber of Commerce
      Designer: J. David Suggs

3442 Burriss Construction Co.
      Designer: J. David Suggs

3443 South Carolina Governors
          Beautification and Improvement Board
      Designer: J. David Suggs

3444 Columbia Urban Service Center
      Designer: J. David Suggs

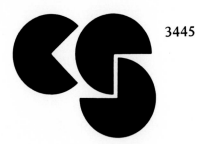 3445

 3449

 3446

 3450

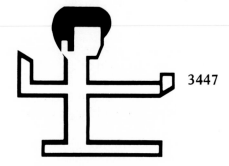 3447

 3451

 3448

3452

3453

3445 Chatham Steel Corporation
Designer: J. David Suggs

3446 Bass Enterprises
Designer: J. David Suggs

3447 Bethleham Community Center
Designer: J. David Suggs

3448 Universal Business Machines Inc.
Designer: J. David Suggs

3449 Dutch Center
Designer: J. David Suggs

3450 Rebel Boat Trailers
Designer: J. David Suggs

3451 South Carolina Commission on
Water Resources
Designer: J. David Suggs

3452 South Carolina Council for Human Rights
Designer: J. David Suggs

3453 Sound Investment
Designer: Michael Pacey/Supergraphics

GreenMark
INCORPORATED

3454

3458

3455

watts
POOL COMPANY

3459

HOUSTON ADVERTISING CLUB

3456

3460

3457

3461

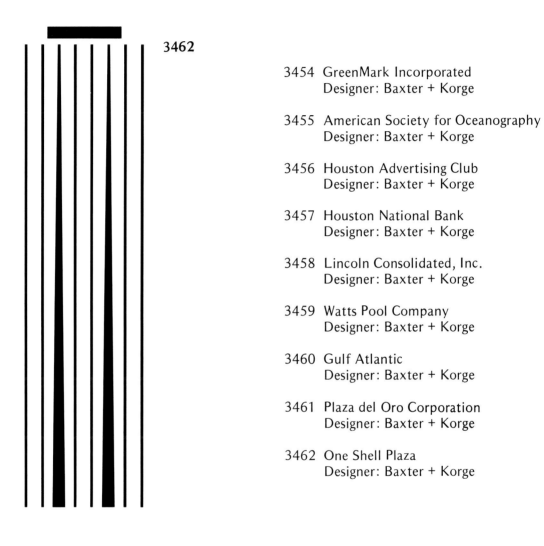

3462

3454 GreenMark Incorporated
Designer: Baxter + Korge

3455 American Society for Oceanography
Designer: Baxter + Korge

3456 Houston Advertising Club
Designer: Baxter + Korge

3457 Houston National Bank
Designer: Baxter + Korge

3458 Lincoln Consolidated, Inc.
Designer: Baxter + Korge

3459 Watts Pool Company
Designer: Baxter + Korge

3460 Gulf Atlantic
Designer: Baxter + Korge

3461 Plaza del Oro Corporation
Designer: Baxter + Korge

3462 One Shell Plaza
Designer: Baxter + Korge

KAMEL'S
WORLD OF TRAVEL, INC.

3463

3465

3466

Mill House

3464

3467

3468

3469

Transco
Companies Inc.

3470

3471

continex

3472

3463 Kamel's World of Travel, Inc.
Designer: Baxter + Korge

3464 Mill House Restaurant, Inc.
Designer: Baxter + Korge

3465 United Services Automobile Association
Designer: Baxter + Korge

3466 Russo Financial Corporation
Designer: Baxter + Korge

3467 Associated Credit Bureaus, Inc.
Designer: Baxter + Korge

3468 Greenway Bank & Trust
Designer: Baxter + Korge

3469 Transco Companies, Inc.
Designer: Baxter + Korge

3470 Anderson Clayton
Designer: Baxter + Korge

3471 Continex
Designer: Baxter + Korge

3472 Mama Rizzo's
Designer: Baxter + Korge

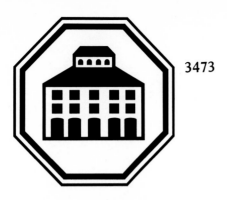 3473

 3477

 3474

 3478

 3473

 3479

 3476

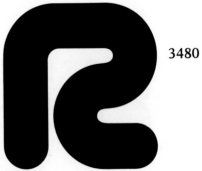 3480

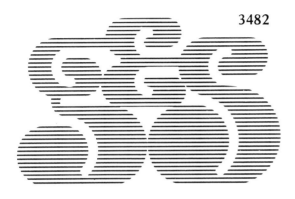

3481

3473 Ohio Village Historic Area
      Designer: Tom Steward

3474 Southeastern Michigan
          Transportation Authority
      Designer: Jac Purdon

3475 Southeastern Michigan
          Transportation Authority
      Designer: Jac Purdon

3476 Community Theatre Assn. of Michigan
      Designer: Jac Purdon

3477 Non Smokers Inc.
      Designer: Jac Purdon

3478 The Bikery
      Designer: Donald Mclean;
          George N. Sepetys & Associates

3479 Homewood Building Company
      Designer: William Davis;
          George N. Sepetys & Associates

3480 Rust-Shield
      Designer: William Davis;
          George N. Sepetys & Associates

3481 Corporate & Association Meeting Services, Inc.
      Designer: Thomas Winberry;
          George N. Sepetys & Associates

3482 G & S Associates, Inc.
      Designer: Thomas Winberry
          George N. Sepetys & Associates

3483 Nylok-Detroit
      Designer: Michael Cromwell;
          George N. Sepetys & Associates

3484 United Skiers Service
      Designer: Michael Cromwell;
          George N. Sepetys & Associates

3482

3483

3484

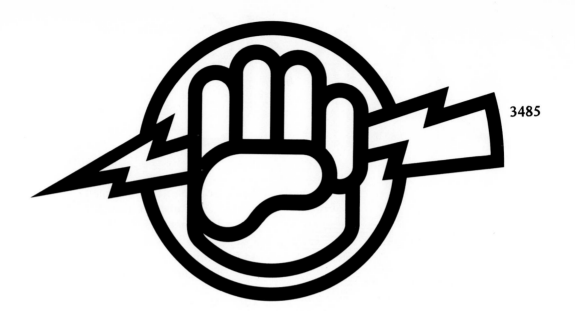

3485

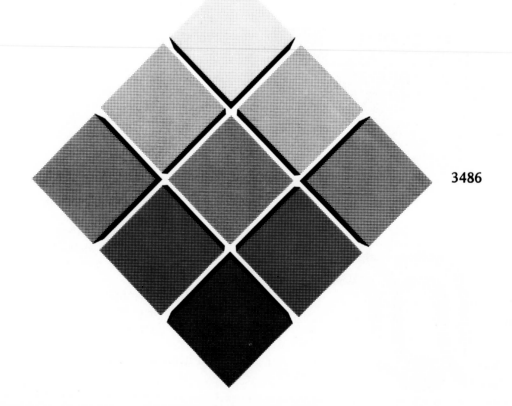

3486

3487

3488

3485 Electrical Contractors Association
      Designer: Donald Mclean;
          George N. Sepetys & Associates

3486 Bruce Crockford, Architect
      Designer: Michael Cromell;
          George N. Sepetys & Associates

3487 Korson's Tree Farms
      Designer: Donald Mclean;
          George N. Sepetys & Associates

3488 Sound-Wave Systems, Inc.
      Designer: Donald Mclean;
          George N. Sepetys & Associates

3489 Travel Center Ski Tours
      Designer: William Davis;
          George N. Sepetys & Associates

3490 Pontiac Stadium Building Authority
      Designer: William Davis;
          George N. Sepetys & Associates

3489

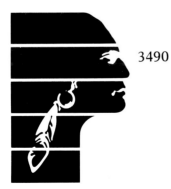

3490

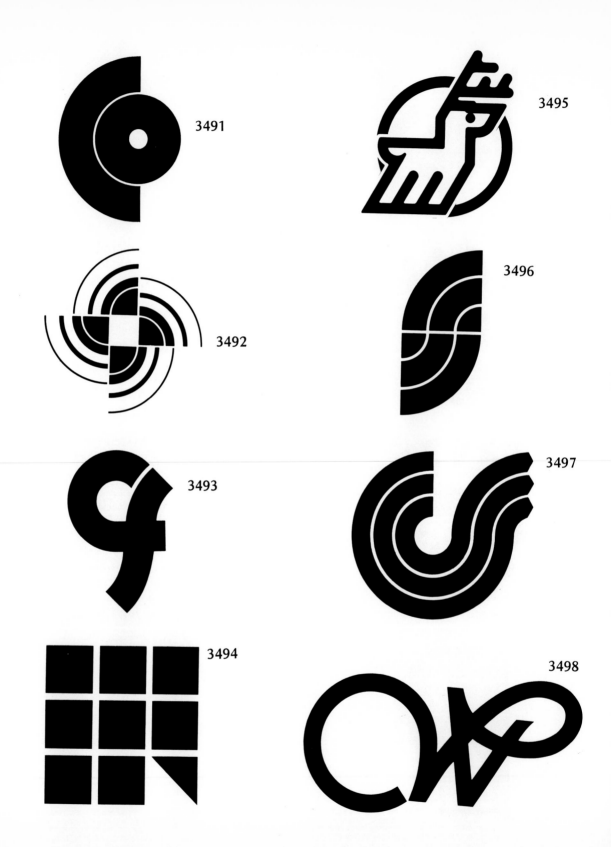

3491

3495

3492

3496

3493

3497

3494

3498

3499

3500

3501

3502

3491 Office Concepts
Designer: William Davis;
George N. Sepetys & Associates

3492 Detroit Suburban Network
Designer: William Davis;
George N. Sepetys & Associates

3493 Glen Flora Country Club
Designer: William Davis;
George N. Sepetys & Associates

3494 The Bill Sandy Co.
Designer: George Sepetys;
George N. Sepetys & Associates

3495 Michigan Stags
Designer: Donald Mclean;
George N. Sepetys & Associates

3496 Somerset Inn
Designer: William Davis;
George N. Sepetys & Associates

3497 J.A. Citrin Sons Company
Designer: William Davis;
George N. Sepetys & Associates

3498 Woodlands
Designer: William Davis;
George N. Sepetys & Associates

3499 The Communication Counsel of America
Designer: Don Weller

3500 Mott Media (for series of books)
Designer: Don Weller

3501 Galleon Productions
Designer: Don Weller/Mark Erickson

3502 Antique Arcade of Beverly Hills
Designer: Don Weller/Bob Maile

 3503

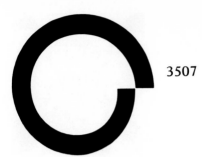 3507

 3504

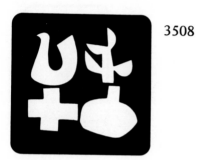 3508

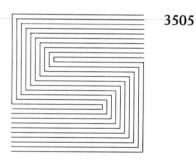 3505

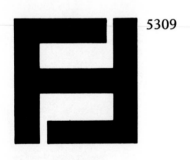 5309

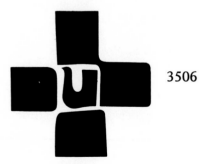 3506

 3510

Geotek incorporated

HAYLOFT TOYS, CRAFTS + COUNTRY CLOTHES 3511

3512

3513

3514

3503 Sports Riders Assn. of Colorado
Designer: Mark Mock

3504 V'Soske
Designer: David Bates

3505 Henry K. Szwarce, Architect
Designer: e. christopher klumb

3506 Benedictine Monks Weston Priory
Designer: e. christopher klumb

3507 Anthony Cipriano Sculpture Studio & Gallery
Designer: e. christopher klumb

3508 Vicovaro Foundation Inc.
Designer: e. christopher klumb

3509 Bruce Fowle/Architect
Designer: e. christopher klumb

3510 Geotek Incorporated
Designer: e. christopher klumb

3511 Hayloft
Designer: e. christopher klumb

3512 IM International
Designer: e. christopher klumb

3513 AIA, Health Facilities Resource Center
Designer: e. christopher klumb

3514 The Tweed Shops
Designer: e. christopher klumb

3515

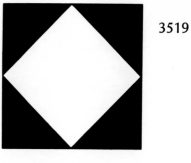

3519

3516

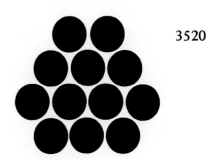

3520

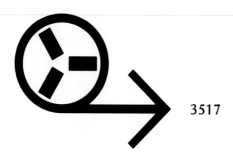

3517

3521

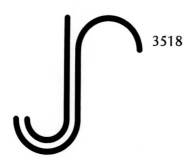

3518

3522

S. BERKOWITZ + ASSOCIATES 3523

3524

3525

3526

3515 Designs by Deborah
      Designer: e. christopher klumb

3516 E. Kohler
      Designer: e. christopher klumb

3517 Nisarc Computers Ltd.
      Designer. e. christopher klumb

3518 Jewelsmiths
      Designer: e. christopher klumb/
      Michael Clemens

3519 Kay Jewelers
      Designer: e. christopher klumb

3520 Intergroup
      Designer: e. christopher klumb

3521 Van Zon International, Inc.
      Designer: e. christopher klumb

3522 Thomas Meacham, Realtor
      Designer: e. christopher klumb/
      Michael Clemens

3523 S. Berkowitz & Associates
      Designer: e. christopher klumb

3524 Intergroup
      Designer: e. christopher klumb

3525 Larousse Inc., USA
      Designer: e. christopher klumb

3526 The Plant Peddler
      Designer: e. christopher klumb

 3527

 3531

 3528

 3532

 3529

 3533

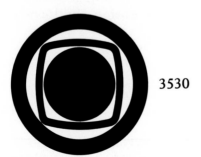 3530

 3534

3535

3536

3537

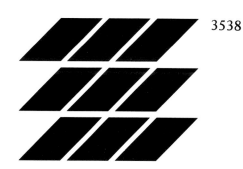

3538

3527 Dallas Museum of Fine Arts
Designer: Crawford Dunn; RYA Graphics, Inc.

3528 Faxon Incorporated
Designer: Crawford Dunn; RYA Graphics, Inc.

3529 The Texas Group
Designer: Crawford Dunn; RYA Graphics, Inc.

3530 WBAP-AM/FM
Designer: Crawford Dunn; RYA Graphics, Inc.

3531 Sands Measurement Corporation
Designer: Crawford Dunn; RYA Graphics, Inc.

3532 North Texas State University
Designer: Crawford Dunn; RYA Graphics, Inc.

3533 Brookhollow Business Park
Designer: Crawford Dunn; RYA Graphics, Inc.

3534 Northlake College
Designer: Crawford Dunn; RYA Graphics, Inc.

3535 Vision Center
Designer: Crawford Dunn; RYA Graphics, Inc.

3536 Lamm-Frates Company
Designer: Crawford Dunn; RYA Graphics, Inc.

3537 Eastland Bank
Designer: Crawford Dunn; RYA Graphics, Inc.

3538 Zale Corporation
Designer: Crawford Dunn/Larry Roberts

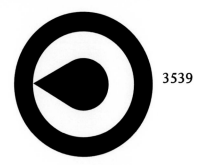 3539

 3543

 3540

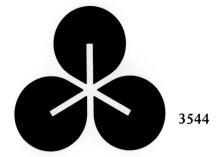 3544

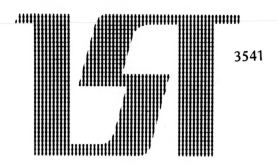 3541

 3545

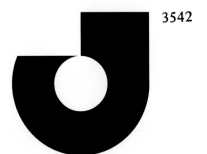 3542

 3546

3547

3548

3549

3550

3539 Westchase Corporation
Designer: Crawford Dunn, RYA Graphics, Inc..

3540 Wilhide Interiors
Designer: Crawford Dunn; RYA Graphics, Inc.

3541 First National Bank of Abilene
Designer: Crawford Dunn; RYA Graphics, Inc.

3542 Grady Jordan & Company
Designer: Crawford Dunn; RYA Graphics, Inc.

3543 Town Center at Chevy Chase
Designer: Crawford Dunn; RYA Graphics, Inc.

3544 Envirodynamics Incorporated
Designer: Crawford Dunn; RYA Graphics, Inc.

3545 Broadnax Printing Company
Designer: Crawford Dunn: RYA Graphics, Inc.

3546 Guardian Savings
Designer: Crawford Dunn; RYA Graphics, Inc.

3547 Campbell Centre
Designer: Crawford Dunn; RYA Graphics, Inc.

3548 Jokari U.S. Inc.
Designer: Crawford Dunn/Harve Hugman

3549 Southern Methodist University
Designer: Crawford Dunn; RYA Graphics, Inc.

3550 Henry C. Beck Company
Designer: Crawford Dunn; RYA Graphics, Inc.

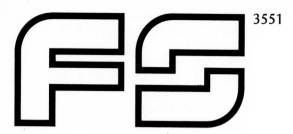 3551

 3555

Texas
Stadium

 3552

3556

**Streams
and
Valleys** 3553

3557

3558

 3554

3559

3560

3561

3562

3551 Fisher & Spellman Architects
Designer: Crawford Dunn

3552 The City of Mesquite, Texas
Designer: Crawford Dunn

3553 Streams and Valleys Commission
Designer: Crawford Dunn

3554 Bank of Commerce
Designer: Crawford Dunn

3555 Texas Stadium
Designer: Crawford Dunn

3556 University of Texas at Arlington
Designer: Crawford Dunn

3557 Ft. Worth Chamber of Commerce
Designer: Crawford Dunn

3558 Deal Development Company
Designer: Crawford Dunn

3559 Dallas Museum of Fine Arts
& Ft. Worth Museum of Art
Designer: Crawford Dunn

3560 Datum Structures Engineers Inc.
Designer: Crawford Dunn

3561 Willow Creek Community Center
Designer: Al Burlini/Tom Morris, Inc.

3562 Lutheran General Hospital
Designer: Al Burlini/Tom Morris, Inc.

 3563

 3567

 3564

 3568

 3565

 3569

 3566

 3570

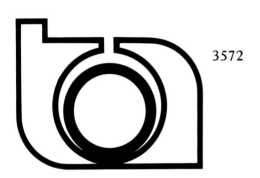

3571

3572

3573

3574

3563 Personalized Service Group
Designer: Al Burlini; Tom Morris Inc.

3564 Young Life
Designer: Al Burlini; Tom Morris, Inc.

3565 Des Plaines National Bank
Designer: Al Burlini; Tom Morris, Inc.

3566 Sur International
Designer: Triad Associates

3567 Cedar Ridge Estates
Designer: Triad Associates

3568 Old Reliable Mortgage Co.
Designer: Triad Associates

3569 Texas Food Merchant
Designer: Triad Associates

3570 Bob Edwards Insurance & Real Estate
Designer: Triad Associates

3571 Our Land, Our Lives . . . a Coalition
for Human Rights
Designer: Triad Associates

3572 Triad Associates
Designer: Triad Associates

3573 The Windmill
Designer: Triad Associates

3574 Hupp Systems, Inc.
Designer: Triad Associates

3575

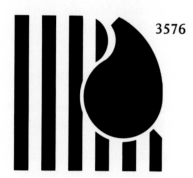

3576

3577

3578

3579

3580

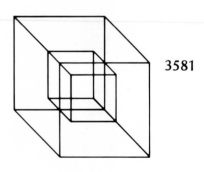

3581

3582

3583

3584

ELK GROVE VILLAGE

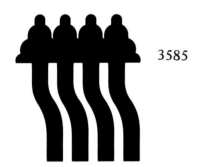

3585

3586

3575 Waco Printing and Stationery Company
      Designer: Triad Associates

3576 Riley's Midway Pharmacy, Inc.
      Designer: Triad Associates

3577 Garden Gate Apartments
      Designer: Triad Associates

3578 Mobile Home Service Co. of the Southwest
      Designer: Triad Associates

3579 TexasBank
      Designer: Triad Associates

3580 One Main Place, Texas Bank
      Designer: The Richards Group

3581 Robert H. Norris, Architect
      Designer: The Richards Group

3582 Exchange Bank
      Designer: The Richards Group

3583 Neuro Systems
      Designer: The Richards Group

3584 Elk Grove Village
      Designer: The Richards Group

3585 The Trails
      Designer: The Richards Group

3586 Varo, Inc.
      Designer: The Richards Group

 3587

 3591

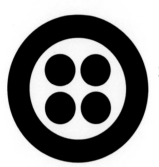 3588

 3592

 3589

 3593

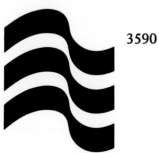 3590

 3594

3595

3596

3597

3598

3587 Cimarron Corporation
Designer: The Richards Group

3588 The Men and Boys Clothing Association
Designer: The Richards Group

3589 Hand Made Originals
Designer: The Richards Group

3590 Chandlers Landing
Designer: The Richards Group

3591 The Backroom Bar
Designer: The Richards Group

3592 The Duffel and Ditty Restaurant
Designer: The Richards Group

3593 Surveyor Companies
Designer: The Richards Group

3594 Lakeside Village
Designer: The Richards Group

3595 Chimney Hill
Designer: The Richards Group

3596 Hillside Townhomes
Designer: The Richards Group

3597 Pinewild Condominiums
Designer: The Richards Group

3598 Channel 8 TV Station
Designer: The Richards Group

 3599

 3603

 3600

 3604

 3601

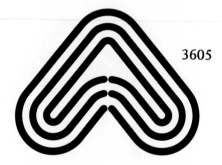 3605

 3602

ESTRADA

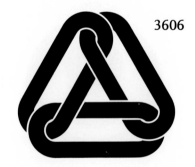 3606

 3607

 3608

 3609

3610

3599 Stoneridge
Designer: The Richards Group

3600 Southern Methodist University
Designer: The Richards Group

3601 Earth Grains Bread
Designer: The Richards Group

3602 Estrada (the wine of Argentina)
Designer: The Richards Group

3603 Jack Unruh
Designer: The Richards Group

3604 USA Film Festival
Designer: The Richards Group

3605 Airborne Connectors
Designer: The Richards Group

3606 Dallas Alliance
Designer: The Richards Group

3607 Neiman Marcus
Designer: The Richards Group

3608 Channel 5 TV Station
Designer: The Richards Group

3609 Dallas Chamber of Commerce
Designer: The Richards Group

3610 Innisgate Townhomes
Designer: The Richards Group

SUMMERTOP 3611

A T N O R T H P A R K

Nitzinger 3612

Dallastyle 3613

THUNDER 3614

3615

3616

3617

3611 Northpark Shopping Center
Designer: The Richards Group

3612 Nitzinger (rock group)
Designer: The Richards Group

3613 Dallas Chamber of Commerce
Designer: The Richards Group

3614 Thunder (rock group)
Designer: The Richards Group

3615 Channel 13 — Educational TV Station
Designer: The Richards Group

3616 James Rutledge (rock singer)
Designer: The Richards Group

3617 Oz Restaurant
Designer: The Richards Group

3618 Earth Grains Bread
Designer: The Richards Group

3618

3619

3623

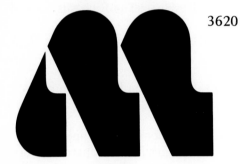

3620

3624

3621

3625

3622

3626

3627

3628

3629

3630

3631

3635

3632

3636

GATX-FULLER

3633

CANDLERIDGE

3637

Bendix

3634

STUD1O

3638

Twin Oaks
HILTON HEAD ISLAND

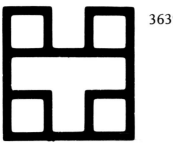 3639

 3640

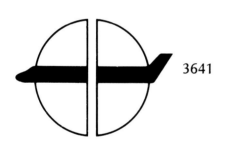 3641

 3642

3631 Union Trust
Designer: The Richards Group

3632 Nevada Cement
Designer: The Richards Group

3633 Candle Ridge
Designer: The Richards Group

3634 Studio Ten Productions, Inc.
Designer: The Richards Group

3635 Equitable Relocation Service
Designer: Equitable Graphics

3636 GATX-Fuller Co.
Designer: Knapp Design Associates

3637 The Bendix Corporation
Designer: Lippincott & Margulies

3638 Twin Oaks Company
Designer: Bruce A. Cottingham

3639 Rhode Island Hospital Trust National Bank
Designer: Agnes Killabin

3640 Archer Daniels Midland Co.
Designer: Latham Tyler Jensen, Inc.

3641 Express International Travel Services
Designer: Mike Quon

3642 Management Research Institute
Designer: Mike Quon

 3643

 3647

 3644

 3648

 3645

 3649

 3646

 3650

 3651

 3652

 3653

 3654

3643 Sentry Medical Products
Designer: Mike Quon

3644 International Geographic Society
Designer: Mike Quon

3645 Vision Institute of America, Inc.
Designer: Richard Howe; Overlock Howe & Co.

3646 Orbon Industries, Inc
Designer: Richard Howe; Overlock Howe & Co.

3647 Goomba's Discotheque
Designer: Richard Deardorff;
Overlock Howe & Co.

3648 Tacony Distributors, Inc.
Designer: Richard Deardorff;
Overlock Howe & Co.

3649 Kalamazoo Center
Designer: Richard Deardorff

3650 Bill's Tap & Restaurant
Designer: Richard Deardorff

3651 St. Joseph High School Swim Club Boosters
Designer: Richard Deardorff

3652 Area Resources Improvement Council
Designer: Richard Deardorff

3653 Highland House Development
Designer: Richard Deardorff

3654 Richard Petrie
Designer: Richard Deardorff

 3655

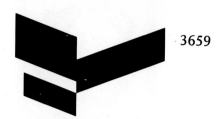 3659

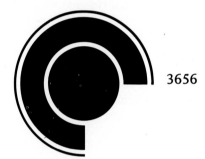 3656

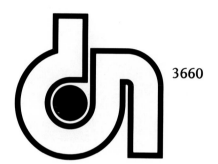 3660

 3657

3661

GALLERY 615 3658

 3662

Lion & The Ram

3663

3664

3665

3666

3655 Tri County Community Action Program
Designer: Richard Deardorff

3656 Industrial Design Center, Whirlpool Corporation
Designer: Richard Deardorff

3657 Twin Cities Area Child Care Center
Designer: Richard Deardorff

3658 Gallery 615
Designer: Richard Deardorff

3659 Retail Marketing Department, Whirlpool Corp.
Designer: Richard Deardorff

3660 Donald Nupp Architectural Services
Designer: Richard Deardorff

3661 Information Center, Whirlpool Corporation
Designer: Richard Deardorff

3662 Lion & The Ram Beauty Salons
Designer: Richard Deardorff

3663 Blossomland United Way
Designer: Richard Deardorff

3664 The Samaritan Center
Designer: Richard Deardorff

3665 Economic & Marketing Research,
       Whirlpool Corporation
Designer: Richard Deardorff

3666 Planned Parenthood of Southwestern Michigan
Designer: Richard Deardorff

3667

3671

3668

3672

3669

3673

3674

3670

3675

3676

3677

3678

3667 Technological Forecast, Whirlpool Corporation
Designer: Richard Deardorff

3668 Project Seed, Whirlpool Corporation
Designer: Richard Deardorff

3669 Grand Mere Association
Designer: Richard Deardorff

3670 American Red Cross Youth
Designer: Richard Deardorff

3671 Benton Harbor/Benton Harbor Township
Model Cities Program
Designer: Richard Deardorff

3672 Edd Gerring
Designer: Richard Deardorff

3673 Southwestern Michigan Regional
Planning Commission
Designer: Richard Deardorff

3674 Patterson Printing
Designer: Richard Deardorff

3675 The Man Alive
Designer: Richard Deardorff

3676 Dwan Graphic Arts
Designer: Richard Deardorff

3677 Town Homes, Inc.
Designer: Richard Deardorff

3678 Wm. E. Mahaffay
Designer: Richard Deardorff

 3679

KAPA 3683

 3680

UNCLES

3684

3681

3685

 3682

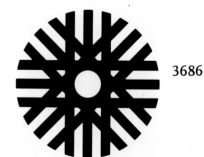 3686

3687

3688

3689

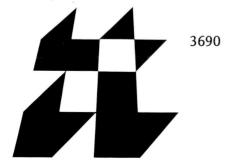

3690

3679 Oxidon 2000 (waste treatment system);
      Whirlpool Corporation
      Designer: Richard Deardorff

3680 St. Joseph, Michigan YMCA
      Designer: Richard Deardorff

3681 Boultinghouse Photography
      Designer: Richard Deardorff

3682 Cathedral School of the Arts
      Designer: Richard Deardorff

3683 Kitchen Appliance Package Assembly;
      Whirlpool Corporation
      Designer: Richard Deardorff

3684 Nadele Alexia O'Donnel
         Marketing Communications
      Designer: Lans Bouthillier;
         Corporate Design Systems

3685 Guidelines
      Designer: Lans Bouthillier;
         Corporate Design Systems

3686 Sun Savings & Loan Association
      Designer: Richard Vieira
         Corporate Design Systems

3687 National Plastifab
      Designer: Lans Bouthillier;
         Corporate Design Systems

3688 Cambridge Historical Commission
      Designer: Richard Vieira;
         Corporate Design Systems

3689 Rockingham Hotel
      Designer: Ronald Couture;
         Corporate Design Systems

3690 Saunders, Cheng & Appleton
      Designer: Richard Vieira;
         Corporate Design Systems

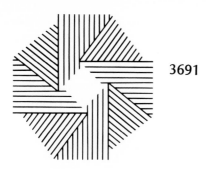 3691

 3695

 3692

 3696

 3693

 3697

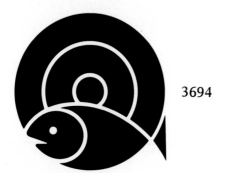 3694

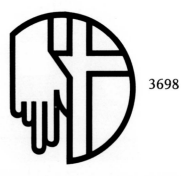 3698

 3699

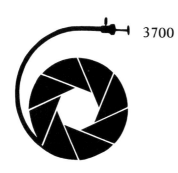 3700

 3701

 3702

3691 Interspace Inc.
Designer: Beverly Gilman;
Corporate Design Systems

3692 World Wildlife Fund
Designer: Lans Bouthillier;
Corporate Design Systems

3693 The Windrifter
Designer: Richard Vieira;
Corporate Design Systems

3694 Outer Banks Safari
Designer: Everett Forbes

3695 Mariner's Cove
Designer: Everett Forbes

3696 Warrington Presbyterian Church
Designer: Everett Forbes

3697 Schwartzschild Jewelers
Designer: Dudley Cook; Martin/Remick/Moore

3698 All Saints Episcopal Church
Designer: Dudley Cook; Martin/Remick/Moore

3699 New Life for Youth
Designer: Dudley Cook; Martin/Remick/Moore

3700 Greg Moore, Photographer
Designer: Dudley Cook; Martin/Remick/Moore

3701 First Mate Restaurants, Inc.
Designer: Jim Lake

3702 American Middle East Consultants
Designer: Jim Lake

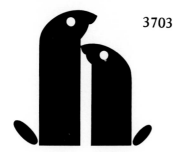

3703

3707

3704

3708

3705

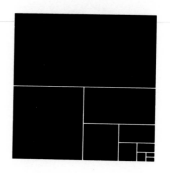

3709

3706

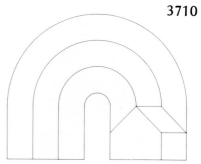

3710

3711

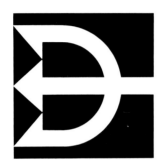

3712

3713

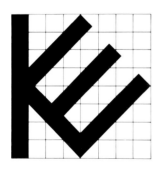

3714

3703 Heimlich & Company
      Designer: Jim Lake

3704 Perky Pet Products, Inc.
      Designer: Jim Lake

3705 Magi-Tack, Inc.
      Designer: Jim Lake

3706 Gemini International
      Designer: Jim Lake

3707 Alco, Inc.
      Designer: Jim Lake

3708 Institute of Trichology
      Designer: The Company

3709 Modular Development Co.
      Designer: The Company

3710 Brentwood Youth House
      Designer: The Company

3711 George Meinzinger Photography
      Designer: The Company

3712 Del Amo Marine
      Designer: The Company

3713 Klein Englander contract furniture sales
      Designer: The Company

3714 Financial Marketing Corporation
      Designer: The Company

3715

3719

3716

3720

3717

3721

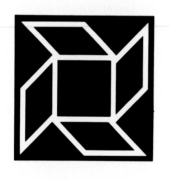

3718

3722

MountainGate

3723

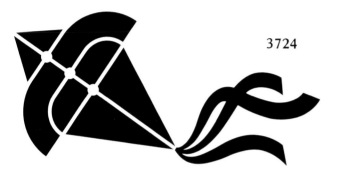

3724

3725

3726

3715 American Telecommunications Corp.
Designer: The Company

3716 Astrodata
Designer: The Company

3717 Allied Corregated Box Corp.
Designer: The Company

3718 Intercontinental Systems
Designer: The Company

3719 Video Security Systems
Designer: The Company

3720 Creative Capital Corporation
Designer: The Company

3721 Al's Garage (clothing)
Designer: Connie Beck;
    John Follis & Associates

3722 Mountaingate Country Club
Designer: Wayne Hunt/Elizabeth Baird;
    John Follis & Associates

3723 Village Palos Verdes
Designer: Wayne Hunt/Connie Beck;
    John Follis & Associates

3724 Village of Woodbridge
Designer: Elizabeth Baird;
    John Follis & Associates

3725 Carolina Copy Center
Designer: Bob Herr; Charles Crone & Assocs.

3726 October Galleries
Designer: Chip Clarke

Tg 3727

 3731

b 3728

 3732

cb 3729

 3733

THE **51** STATE 3730

CHANNEL **13**

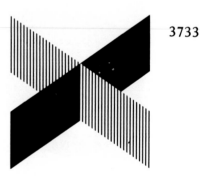 3734

3735

3736

3737

3727 Texasgulf Inc.
Designer: George Tscherny

3728 R.L. Banks & Associates, Inc.
Designer: George Tscherny

3729 Curtis Brown Ltd.
Designer: George Tscherny

3730 Educational Broadcasting Co.
Designer: George Tscherny

3731 Michael A. Schacht Inc.
Designer: George Tscherny

3732 Setec — Weidlinger
Designer: George Tscherny

3733 Design Built Exhibits, Inc.
Designer: George Tscherny

3734 Community Vasectomy Clinic
Designer: Ed Penniman

3735 The Wheel Works (pottery)
Designer: Ed Penniman

3736 Todd Thal (Mercedes-Benz repair)
Designer: Ed Penniman

3737 Victor Kemp Company
Designer: Ed Penniman

3738 Center on Aging
Designer: Calvin Woo

3738

3739

3743

3744

3740

3741

3745

3742

3746

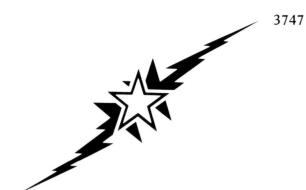

3747

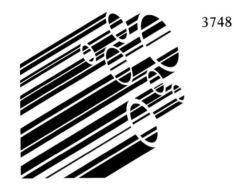

3748

3739 La Jolla Development Company
Designer: Calvin Woo

3740 Woo Chee Chong, Inc. (oriental foods)
Designer: Calvin Woo

3741 Grossmont Hospital
Designer: Calvin Woo

3742 Shared Jobs
Designer: Calvin Woo

3743 About Behavior Change Groups
Designer: Calvin Woo

3744 Arizona Brake & Clutch, Inc.
Designer: Calvin Woo

3745 Best Photo
Designer: Calvin Woo

3746 W & M Plastics, Inc.
Designer: Calvin Woo

3747 Starr Boltt, youth fashions
Designer: Calvin Woo

3748 Dial Tube Company
Designer: Patrick Benton

3749 Patrick Benton Advertising Design
Designer: Patrick Benton

3750 The Art Club News
Designer: Patrick Benton

3749

3750

The Art Club News

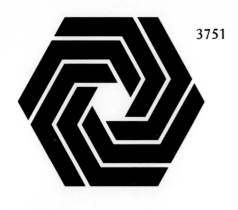

3751

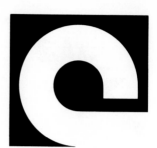

3752

3756

3753

3757

3754

3758

3759

3760

3761

3762

3751 American Commonwealth Financial Corp.
Designer: Patrick Benton

3752 KTLC Radio
Designer: Patrick Benton

3753 Splinter Pickle Co., Inc.
Designer: Victor DiCristo

3754 Cedarburg Recycling Program
Designer: Victor DiCristo

3755 Commercial Bank
Designer: Victor DiCristo

3756 DiCristo Design
Designer: Victor DiCristo

3757 Children's Service Soceity of Wisconsin
Designer: Victor DiCristo

3758 Madison Newspapers, Inc.
Designer: Victor DiCristo

3759 Freed's Stores
Designer: L.S. Krispinsky

3760 Executive Advertising
Designer: L.S. Krispinsky

3761 Academic Improvement Center
Designer: Don Primi

3762 Gabor J. Mertl & Assocs., Architects
Designer: Don Primi

3763

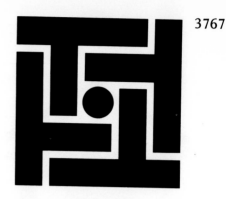

3767

3764

3768

3765

3769

3766

3770

3771

3772

3773

3774

 3775

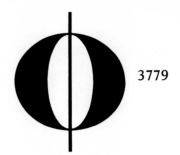 3779

 3776

 3780

 3777

3781

3777

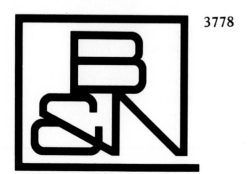 3778

 3782

3783

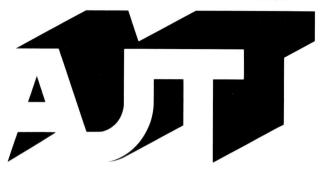

3784

3785

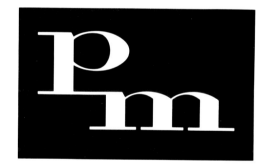

3786

3775 Zale Realty Corp.
Designer: Don Primi

3776 Carol Bachman, Interior Design
Designer: Don Primi

3777 Louis Vynerib & Associates, Inc.
Designer: Don Primi

3778 Blum & Nerzig, Architects
Designer: Don Primi

3779 Phi Equities Corp.
Designer: Don Primi

3780 Quakertown Brick & Tile Co., Inc.
Designer: Don Primi

3781 Victory Corporation
Designer: Don Primi

3782 Credit Card Exchange
Designer: Don Primi

3783 Arthur J. Taft Co.
Designer: Don Primi

3784 Compac, Inc.
Designer: Don Primi

3785 Perry Meyers, Inc.
Designer: Don Primi

3786 Property Management Associates, Inc.
Designer: Don Primi

3787

3788

3789

3790

3791

Cherokee Brick

3792

3793

ARLEY PROPERTIES COMPANY

3794

SYSCON

3787 Trans-Ad, Ltd.
      Designer: Don Primi

3788 Target Rock Corporation
      Designer: Don Primi

3789 Penn-State Corporation
      Designer: Don Primi

3790 Leisure Distributors, Inc.
      Designer: Don Primi

3791 Cherokee Brick Co. of North Carolina
      Designer: Don Primi

3792 Tele-Communications Consultants, Inc.
      Designer: Don Primi

3793 Arley Properties Co.
      Designer: Don Primi

3794 Syscon Corporation
      Designer: Don Primi

3795

3796

3799

3797

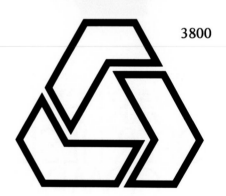

3800

3798

INTERLOC

 3801

 3802

 3803

3804

3795 Evans Clay Products, Inc.
Designer: Don Primi

3796 Lee A. Sagistano, AIA Architect
Designer: Don Primi

3797 Michael Harris Spector & Assocs., Architects
Designer: Don Primi

3798 Interloc Realty Co.
Designer: Don Primi

3799 Bamberger Polymers, Inc.
Designer: Don Primi

3800 Triangle Brick Co.
Designer: Don Primi

3801 David Manufacturing Co.
Designer: David M. Murphy

3802 Southeast Ohio Emergency Medical Services
Designer: Dean R. Lindsay

3803 Dairy Council of Georgia, Inc.
Designer: Judy Gazaway; Atvur Associates

3804 Pinewood Plantation
Designer: Savas Atvur; Atvur Associates

3805

3809

3806

3810

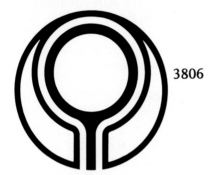

3807

3811

3808

3812

STOTTER 3813

3814

FISCHER X·RAY 3815

3816

 3817

the cheese shop

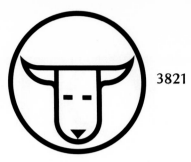 3821

the meat market

 3818

the international café

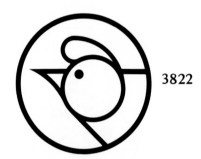 3822

the poultry market

 3819

the cooking counter

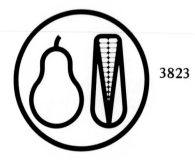 3823

the produce market

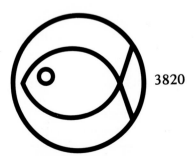 3820

the fish market

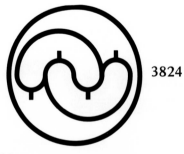 3824

the sausage shop

Treetops 3825

3826

3827

3817–3824 Series of symbols for
Market Place
Designer: Anthony Aviles;
Harper + George

3825 Treetops Condominiums
Designer: Anthony Aviles;
Harper + George

3826 Jonynas and Shephard, Stained
Glass Window Designers
Designer: Anthony Aviles;
Harper + George

3827 Marvil Gelman, Lighting Consultant
Designer: Anthony Aviles;
Harper + George

3828 New York State Democtatic 1974
Fund Raising Committee
Designer: Anthony Aviles;
Harper + George

3828

Coffee Garden 3829

3833

Pool Deck 3830

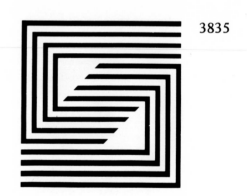

3834

Health Club 3831

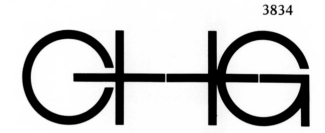

3835

3832

3836

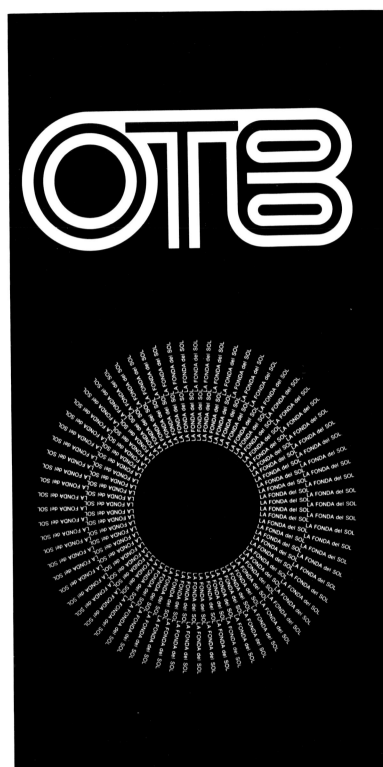

3839

3843

3840

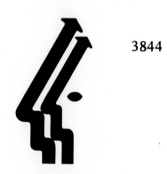

3844

3841

3845

3841

3846

EverFlex 3847

3848

3849

3850

3851

3855

3852

3856

3853

3857

3854

3858

**Western Pacific
Financial Corporation**

3859

3860

3861

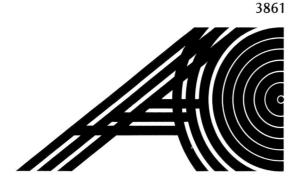

3862

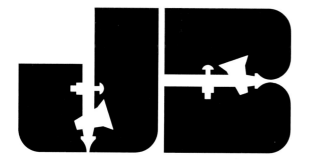

3851 Interim, Inc.
Designer: Gale William Ikola

3852 Don G. Lee and Associates
Designer: Gale William Ikola

3853 Special Blue Dot Springs
Designer: Gale William Ikola

3854 Minnesota Zoological Society
Designer: Gale William Ikola

3855 F & M Savings Bank
Designer: Gale William Ikola

3856 Shippers Supply Co.
Designer: Jack E. Kannapell, Jr.

3857 Mockingbird Valley Racquet Club
Designer: Jack E. Kannapell, Jr.

3858 Western Pacific Financial Corporation
Designer: Mike Kaiser

3859 Decision 75 — Sherman Oaks Lutheran Church
Designer: Daniel M. Partain

3860 Redd Foxx Productions
Designer: Daniel M. Partain

3861 Audio Tek (recording studio)
Designer: Cyril John Schlosser

3862 Jim Burns (airbrush specialist)
Designer: Cyril John Schlosser

3863

type

3867

3864

3868

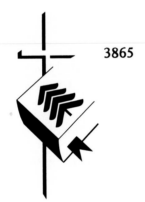

3865

3869

Immanuel Baptist Church

3866

PHOENIX
CIVIC PLAZA

3670

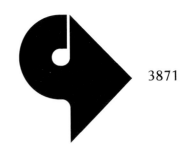

3871

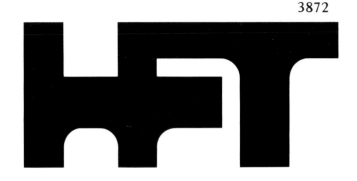

3872

3873

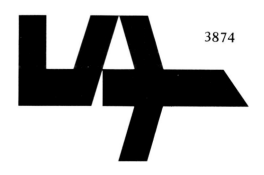

3874

3863 Northeast Residence, Inc.
      Designer: Cyril John Schlosser

3864 Dietrich Company
      Designer: Cyril John Schlosser

3865 Sierra School of the Bible
      Designer: Don Sterrenburg

3866 Immanuel Baptist Church
      Designer: Don Sterrenburg

3867 Compugraphic Corporation, Type Div.
      Designer: Don Sterrenburg

3868 Cedar Creek Festival of Arts & Crafts
      Designer: Victor DiCristo

3869 Jack Burktenica/Landscape Architect
      Designer: Ernest H. Stedman;
          E.H. Stedman Graphic Design

3870 Phoenix Civic Plaza
      Designer: Ernest H. Stedman;
          E.H. Stedman Graphic Design

3871 Cooper Architectural Signs
      Designer: Ernest H. Stedman;
          E.H. Stedman Graphic Design

3872 Howard F. Thompson, Architect
      Designer: Ernest H. Stedman;
          E.H. Stedman Graphic Design

3873 Pacific Design Center
      Designer: Ernest H. Stedman;
          Rex Goode Organization for Design

3874 Los Angeles International Airport
      Designer: Ernest H. Stedman;
          E.H. Stedman Graphic Design

3875

3879

3876

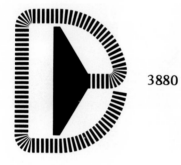

3880

3877

3881

3878

3882

3883

3884

3885

3886

3875 Sequoia Pacific
    Designer: Ken Chapman;
        Rex Goode Organization for Design

3876 Yamaha Learn to Ride Program
    Designer: Carlos Huerta/Roger Johnson;
        Huerta Design

3877 Design Communications
    Designer: Roger Johnson; Huerta Design

3878 Asanuma
    Designer: Roger Johnson; Huerta Design

3879 The Art Group
    Designer: Roger Johnson; Huerta Design

3880 Doyle Group
    Designer: Roger Johnson; Huerta Design

3881 National Credit Information Services
    Designer: Jim Potocki; Huerta Design

3882 Cornell Bridgers & Troller
    Designer: Roger Johnson; Huerta Design

3883 International Cycle House
    Designer: Carlos Huerta/Roger Johnson;
        Huerta Design

3884 Arroyo Foods
    Designer: Roger Johnson; Huerta Design

3885 Extended Care Facilities, Inc.
    Designer: Roger Johnson; Huerta Design

3886 Knott's Berry Farm
    Designer: Carlos Huerta/Roger Johnson;
        Huerta Design

SIDE STREET

3887

3888

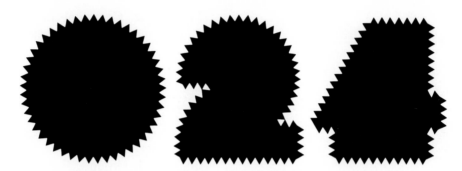

3889

3890

3891

3892

3893

3887 Giannelli
Designer: Carlos Huerta; Huerta Design

3888 Art Directors Club of Los Angeles
Designer: Roger Johnson; Huerta Design

3889 Watson Industrial Center
Designer: Octavio Huerta/Roger Johnson;
Huerta Design

3890 Tyco Industries
Designer: Hector Huerta/Roger Johnson;
Huerta Design

3891 Statakil Corporation
Designer: Roger Johnson; Huerta Design

3892 Pioneer French Baking Co.
Designer: Roger Johnson; Huerta Design

3893 Huerta Design Associates
Designer: Hector Huerta/Roger Johnson;
Huerta Design

3894 Liquidity Fund, Inc.
Designer: Jim Potocki; Huerta Design

3894

 3895

 3899

 3896

 3900

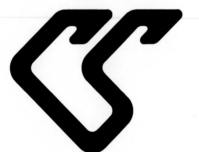 3897

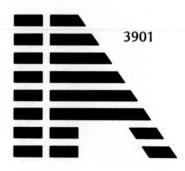 3901

 3898

3902

3903

3904

3895 Bob Crane & Assocs., Realtor
      Designer: Jim Potocki; Jim Potocki & Assocs.

3896 Ross Loos Medical Group
      Designer: Carlos Huerta/Roger Johnson;
          Huerta Design

3897 E. Clark Starr, Graphic Design
      Designer: E. Clark Starr

3898 The Galleon & Gallery Ltd.
      Designer: E. Clark Starr

3899 American Sawing and Drilling Co., Inc.
      Designer: E. Clark Starr

3900 New England Alumni Trust
      Designer: E. Clark Starr

3901 Input Applications Inc.
      Designer: E. Clark Starr

3902 Team Marketing Corporation
      Designer: E. Clark Starr

3903 The Killdear Society
      Designer: Elaine M. Lyerly;
          Monte J. Curry Marketing

3904 Exhibit World, Inc.
      Designer: Monte J. Curry

3905 Nathaniel Hill and Associates
      Designer: Monte J. Curry

3905

3906

3910

DIAL·A·RECIPE

3907

Layne

3911

the BeaHive

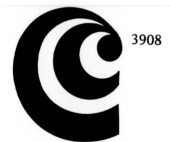
3908

3912

3909

englewood
Pride in its People

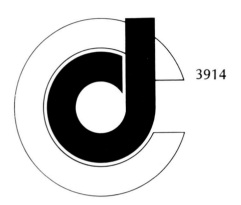

HUK·A·P∞ 3913

3914

3915

The Family Bank

3916

3906 News Release Service
Designer: Elaine M. Lyerly

3907 Layne-Trane Service
Designer: Monte J. Curry

3908 Caralou Callissi Cirillo, Interior Designer
Designer: Kay Ritta

3909 Englewood (city symbol)
Designer: Kay Ritta

3910 Dial-A-Recipe
Designer: Kay Ritta

3911 The BeaHive
Designer: Kay Ritta

3912 Englewood Independent Alliance
Designer: Kay Ritta

3913 Huk-A-Poo
Designer: Kay Ritta

3914 Circle D
Designer: Paul Turzio

3915 The Family Bank
Designer: John H. Harland Co.

3916 Granite City Bank
Designer: John H. Harland Co.

3917

Family Financial Center

3921

3918

3922

3919

3923

3920

3924

3925

3926

3917 Bank of Clarksdale
      Designer: John H. Harland Co.

3918 North St. Louis Trust Co.
      Designer: John H. Harland Co.

3919 Vic Womack & Associates, Inc.
      Designer: Point Communications, Inc.

3920 Laver-Emerson Fun'Set Vacations
      Designer: Point Communications, Inc.

3921 Rod Laver's LET/SET Resorts, Inc.
      Designer: Point Communications, Inc.

3922 American Assn. of Real Estate Boards, Inc.
      Designer: David Rainey

3923 The College of Cosmetology
      Designer: David Rainey

3924 The Great American Pant Co.
      Designer: David Rainey

3925 Steve Altman Photography
      Designer: David Rainey

3926 Mentor, Inc., Financial Consultants
      Designer: David Rainey

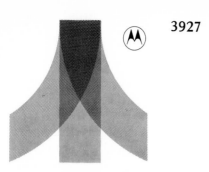 3927

 3931

 3928

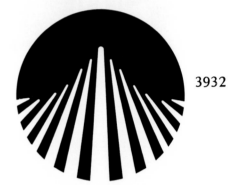 3932

 3929

JETARAMA THEATER

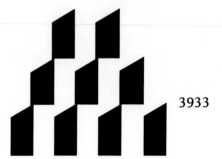 3933

 3930

 3934

MIRROR **3935**

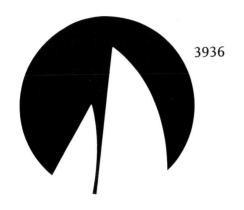

3936

3937

3938

3927 Motorola, Inc./Quasar
Designer: Visual Design Center, Inc.

3928 General Biologicals Co.
Designer: Visual Design Center, Inc.

3929 United Airlines Jetarama Theater
Designer: Visual Design Center, Inc.

3930 J.A. Olson Co.
Designer: Visual Design Center, Inc.

3931 Walter Frank Organization
Designer: Visual Design Center, Inc.

3932 Baldwin & Howell Companies
Designer: Michael Vanderbyl

3933 Hogland & Bogart
Designer: Michael Vanderbyl

3934 KTVU, Channel 2
Designer: Michael Vanderbyl/Dean Smith

3935 Transamerica Corp. (for employee magazine)
Designer: Michael Vanderbyl

3936 Mitchell Sails
Designer: Michael Vanderbyl

3937 AMCOM
Designer: Michael Vanderbyl

3938 Environmental Measurements
Designer: Michael Vanderbyl

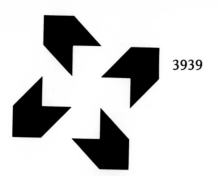 3939

 3943

 3940

 3944

 3941

 3945

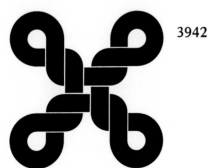 3942

 3946

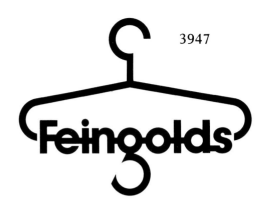

3947

3948

3949

3950

3939 Hospital Consortium, Inc.
      Designer: Michael Vanderbyl

3940 The Tischer Company
      Designer: Michael Vanderbyl

3941 Alpine Villa Development Co.
      Designer: Michael Vanderbyl

3942 The Yachtsmans Exchange
      Designer: Michael Vanderbyl

3943 Five Star Insurance Plan
      Designer: Jim Maccaroni; Parker Allen Co., Inc.

3944 Advertising Typographers
      Designer: Jim Maccaroni; Parker Allen Co., Inc.

3945 Economic Counselors, Inc.
      Designer: Philip Sehenuk; Parker Allen Co., Inc.

3946 Kragwood Broadcasting Inc.
      Designer: Doug Powell; Image Group

3947 Feingolds Mens Wear
      Designer: Doug Powell; Image Group

3948 Recreational Environments Consultants
      Designer: Doug Powell; Image Group

3949 Jerry's of Chico
      Designer: Charles Osborn; Image Group

3950 Health Manpower Council, Northeastern Calif.
      Designer: Charles Osborn/Donald Price;
          Image Group

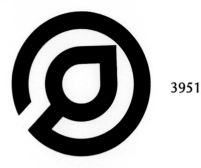 3951

 3955

 3952

 3956

 3953

 3957

 3954

 3958

3959

XANDOR

3960

DESIGN DEPOT
TREASTER & GREEN

3961

3962

 3963

 3967

 3964

3968

3965

3969

3966

COMMUNITY/CONVENTION CENTER

3970

3971

3972

3973

3974

3963 Calif. Div. of Tourism Development
Designer: Gaylord Bennitt/
Ted Thames

3964 Buffalo Brewing Co.
Designer: John Gregg Berryman/
Gaylord Bennitt

3965 Norwood Village
Designer: Doug Powell; Image Group

3966 Sacramento Convention Center
Designer: Gaylord Bennitt/Steve Madeira

3967 Sportsden
Designer: G. Bennitt/J.G. Berryman

3968 Sacramento Amer. Rev. Bicentennial
Designer: Gaylord Bennitt

3969 Johnston & Murphy Shoe Co.
Designer: Brad Whitfield; Design Graphics

3970 Hospital Corp. of America, Intl. Division
Designer: Hermann F. Zimmermann
Design Graphics

3971 Nashville Musical Instruments Co.
Designer: Bill Dick; Design Graphics

3972 Cromwell and Co.
Designer: Bill Dick; Design Graphics

3973 Horace Small Co.
Designer: Hermann F. Zimmermann;
Design Graphics

3974 Johnston & Murphy Shoe Co.
Designer: Brad Whitfield; Design Graphics

3975

3976

3977

3978

3979

3980

3981

3975 Prince Street Gallery
      Designer: Gene Krackehl

3976 San Francisco Municipal Railway
      Designer: Landor Associates

3977 Montedison Group
      Designer: Landor Associates

3978 Industria Italiana Petroli
      Designer: Landor Associates

3979 Dynic Corporation
      Designer: Landor Associates

3980 San Miguel Corporation
      Designer: Landor Associates

3981 Euromercato
      Designer: Landor Associates

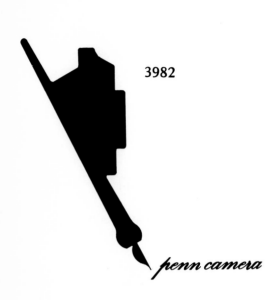

3982

penn camera

3985

court clothes

3986

3983

3987

USFundingCorporation

3984

Citizens for Highway Safety

3988

The COUNTRY COBBLER

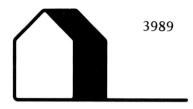

3989

3990

3991

3982 Penn Camera
       Designer: John G. Cutler

3983 Travel-Van Camper
       Designer: John G. Cutler

3984 Citizens for Highway Safety
       Designer: Gray Whyte Design House, Inc.

3985 North Jersey Blood Center
       Designer: Gray Whyte Design House, Inc.

3986 Court Clothes, Ltd.
       Designer: Gray Whyte Design House, Inc.

3987 US Funding Corporation
       Designer: Gray Whyte Design House, Inc.

3988 The Country Cobbler
       Designer: Gray Whyte Design House, Inc.

3989 Gray Whyte Design House, Inc.
       Designer: Gray Whyte Design House, Inc.

3990 Tyo Publishers
       Designer: Pat Taylor, Inc.

3991 Carley Capital Group, Inc.
       Designer: Pat Taylor, Inc.

3992 Airy View Condominium
       Designer: Pat Taylor, Inc.

3992

3993

3997

3994

AFTER LOVE® TOWELETTES

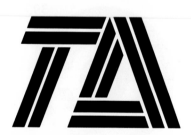
3998

The Plant'n Pot Shop

3995

TA
3999

3996

OPTICOMP

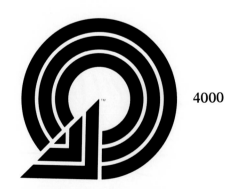
4000

4001

4002

4003

4004

3993 Urban Land Perspectives, Inc.
      Designer: Pat Taylor, Inc.

3994 After Love Towelettes
      Designer: Pat Taylor, Inc.

3995 Dana Research Inc.
      Designer: Pat Taylor, Inc.

3996 Opticomp
      Designer: Pat Taylor, Inc.

3997 Addario Design Associates
      Designer: Addario Design Associates

3998 The Plant 'n Pot Shop
      Designer: Addario Design Associates

3999 Trend Associates, Inc.
      Designer: Addario Design Associates

4000 Red Ball Express
      Designer: Addario Design Associates

4001 Airport Community Relations
      Designer: Wm Spivey Design

4002 For Sale by Owner
      Designer: Wm Spivey Design

4003 Jack Ramsey Communications
      Designer: Wm Spivey Design

4004 Sarie Hylkema
      Designer: Wm Spivey Design

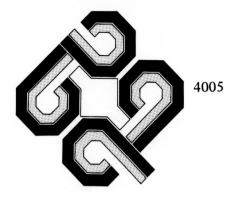

4005

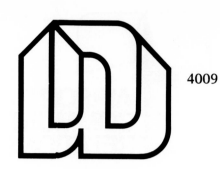

4009

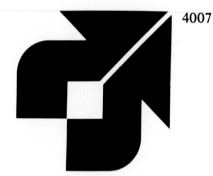

4006

Banco de Venezuela

4010

4007

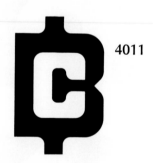

4011

4008

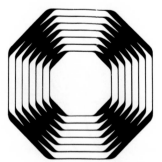

4012

4013

4014

4015

arquitectura
BECKHOFF

4016

4005 John Bates Architects
Designer: Wm Spivey Design

4006 Wm Spivey Design
Designer: Wm Spivey Design

4007 Promotora Venezolano Alemana
Designer: Jesus Emilio Franco

4008 Mini Drug
Designer: Jesus Emilio Franco

4009 Nancy Wilson - personal
Designer: Jesus Emilio Franco

4010 Banco de Venezuela
Designer: Jesus Emilio Franco

4011 Banco de Comercio
Designer: Jesus Emilio Franco

4012 C.A. La Electricidad de Caracas
Designer: Jesus Emilio Franco

4013 Villas del Mar
Designer: Jesus Emilio Franco

4014 Crenca
Designer: Jesus Emilio Franco

4015 Arquitectura Beckhoff
Designer: Jesus Emilio Franco

4016 Banco Provincial
Designer: Jesus Emilio Franco

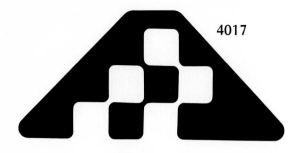

4017

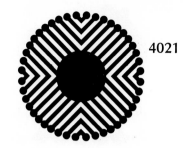

4021

4018

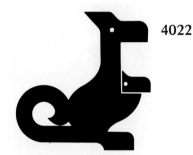

4022

TENSIDOR

4019

4023

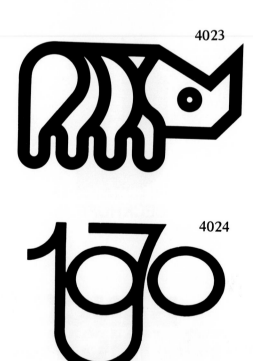

4020

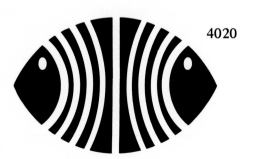

4024

4025

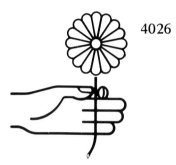

4026

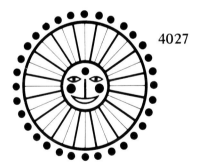

4027

4028

4017 La Piramide
Designer: Jesus Emilio Franco

4018 Caracas 400 Anos
Designer: Jesus Emilio Franco

4019 Tensidor
Designer: Jesus Emilio Franco

4020 Camuri Mar
Designer: Jesus Emilio Franco

4021 Primer Congreso de Medicina Interna
Designer: Jesus Emilio Franco

4022 Vivica
Designer: Jesus Emilio Franco

4023 Vigilancia y Transportes de Seguridad
Designer: Jesus Emilio Franco

4024 Calendario Grey's
DEsigner: Jesus Emilio Franco

4025 Prado Guayana
Designer: Jesus Emilio Franco

4026 Humanizacion de Caracas
Designer: Jesus Emilio Franco

4027 Leche los Teques
Designer: Jesus Emilio Franco

4028 Onda Nueva
Designer: Jesus Emilio Franco

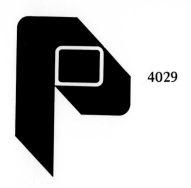

4029

4030

4033

4034

4031

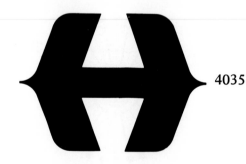

4035

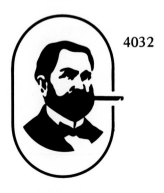

4032

4036

4037

4038

4039

4040

4029 Produzco
Designer: Jesus Emilio Franco

4030 Prado Humboldt
Designer: Jesus Emilio Franco

4031 Banc Obrero
Designer: Jesus Emilio Franco

4032 Tobacos La Cumanesa
Designer: Jesus Emilio Franco

4033 Empaques Clement
Designer: Jesus Emilio Franco

4034 Parques & Recreacion
Designer: Jesus Emilio Franco

4035 Hideca
Designer: Jesus Emilio Franco

4036 Centro Simon Bolivar
Designer: Jesus Emilio Franco

4037 Arca-Centro Comercial
Designer: Jesus Emilio Franco

4038 Los Desarollistas
Designer: Jesus Emilio Franco

4039 San Felipe
Designer: Jesus Emilio Franco

4040 Caribbean Hotel
Designer: Jesus Emilio Franco

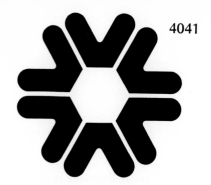

4041

4045

4042

4046

4043

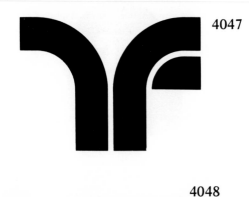

4047

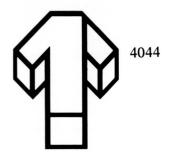

4044

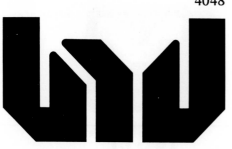

4048

4049

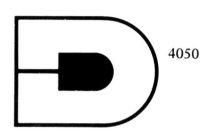

4050

4051

4052

4041 Minesterio de Obras Publicas
Designer: Jesus Emilio Franco

4042 Pata Pata — Zapateria
Designer: Jesus Emilio Franco

4043 Novgorod — Restaurant
Designer: Jesus Emilio Franco

4044 Tecnica Uno
Designer: Jesus Emilio Franco

4045 Productora de Grasas — El Dorado
Designer: Jesus Emilio Franco

4046 Solcasa
Designer: Jesus Emilio Franco

4047 Technical Financing
Designer: Jesus Emilio Franco

4048 Banco Nacional de Descuento
Designer: Jesus Emilio Franco

4049 Avicine
Designer: Jesus Emilio Franco

4050 Ernesto D'escrivan
Designer: Jesus Emilio Franco

4051 Automercados Global
Designer: Jesus Emilio Franco

4052 Banco Hipotecario del Este
Designer: Jesus Emilio Franco

 4053

 4057

 4054

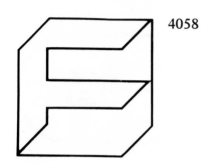 4058

 4055

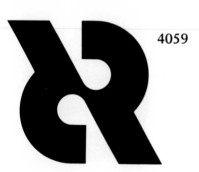 4059

 4056

 4060

4061

4062

4063

4064

4053 Capra
Designer: Jesus Emilio Franco

4054 Clement
Designer: Jesus Emilio Franco

4055 Centro Villasmal
Designer: Jesus Emilio Franco

4056 Viveros Urimare
Designer: Jesus Emilio Franco

4057 Optica Caracas
Designer: Jesus Emilio Franco

4058 Forum
Designer: Jesus Emilio Franco

4059 Rendimax
Designer: Jesus Emilio Franco

4060 Glu Glu
Designer: Jesus Emilio Franco

4061 La Floresta — Instuto Medico
Designer: Jesus Emilio Franco

4062 Golden House
Designer: Jesus Emilio Franco

4063 Centro Comercial Chacaito
Designer: Jesus Emilio Franco

4064 Air Parts
Designer: Jesus Emilio Franco

4065

4069

4066

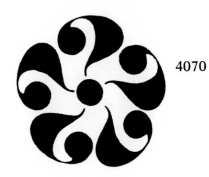

4070

4067

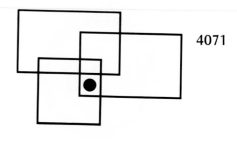

4071

4068

4072

4073

4074

Waugh Controls 4075

4076

4065 Andres Rosa - Personal
Designer: Jesus Emilio Franco

4066 Northeast Regional Center for
Rural Development — Cornell Univ.
Designer: James Estes

4067 Dept. of Human Development & Family
Studies — Cornell University
Designer: James Estes

4068 Graphic Productions
Designer: Cutro Associates

4069 Essex Lighting Co.
Designer: Cutro Associates

4070 How Graphics, Inc.
Designer: Cutro Associates

4071 Amber Aluminium Co.
Designer: Cutro Associates

4072 Happiness Launders & Dry Cleaners
Designer: Tim Oei Ing King

4073 Oei Ing King Design
Designer: Tim Oei Ing King

4074 Seven Enterprises Ltd.
Designer: Tim Oei Ing King

4075 Waugh Controls
Designer: Charles C. Waugh

4076 Blalack, Loop & Townsend
Designer: Stan Hutchinson;
Selje, Bond & Stewart

 4077

 4081

 4078

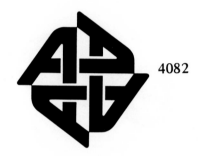 4082

 4079

 4083

 4080

 4084

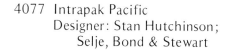

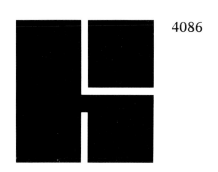

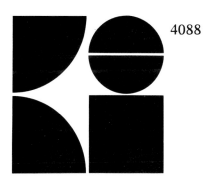

4077   Intrapak Pacific
      Designer: Stan Hutchinson;
         Selje, Bond & Stewart

4078   Ten Downing Restaurant
      Designer: Stan Hutchinson;
         Selje, Bond & Stewart

4079   The Ben Jonson Restaurant (Lawry's)
      Designer: Stu Denker; Selje, Bond & Stewart

4080   The Chronicle Restaurant
      Designer: Gary Moore; Selje, Bond & Stewart

4081   Architectural Woodworking Co.
      Designer: Stan Hutchinson/Skip Morrow;
         Selje, Bond & Stewart

4082   Applewhite Mortgage Co.
      Designer: Skip Morrow;
         Selje, Bond & Stewart

4083   Nichols Family
      Designer: Larry Nichols;
         Emerson/Franzke Advertising, Inc.

4084   Kansas Power & Light Co., 50th Anniversary
      Designer: Larry Nichols;
         Emerson/Franzke Advertising, Inc.

4085   The Jockey Club
      Designer: Larry Nichols;
         Emerson/Franzke Advertising, Inc.

4086   Hester Industries, Inc.
      Designer: Randall R. Roth

4087   Stuermer, Architect
      Designer: Randall R. Roth

4088   Kiwanis International
      Designer: Randall R. Roth

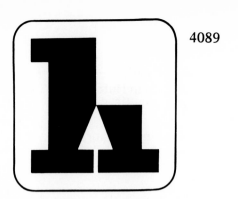 4089

 4093

American Trauma Society

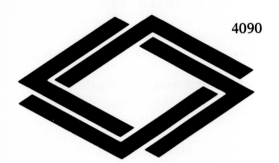 4090

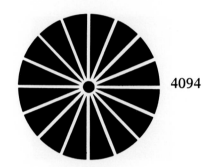 4094

 4091

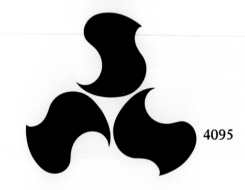 4095

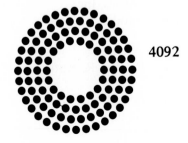 4092

 4096

4097

CHARLESTON. SOUTH CAROLINA

4098

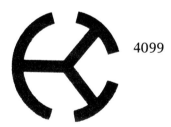

4099

4100

4089 Hardacre Real Estate
Designer: Randall R. Roth

4090 Diamond Rubber Products, Inc.
Designer: Don Davis Design

4091 Don Davis Design
Designer: Don Davis Design

4092 Quincy's 23rd Annual Art Show
Designer: Don Davis Design

4093 American Trauma Society
Designer: Dennis Ichiyama

4094 Tokyo International Airport
Designer: Dennis Ichiyama

4095 Radio WYEP
Designer: Dennis Ichiyama

4096 Tenco Enterprises
Designer: Dennis Ichiyama

4097 Charleston County Public Schools
Charleston, South Carolina

4098 First National Bank of Clearwater
Designer: Ensslin Advertising Agency

4099 Equity Oil Co.
Designer: J. P. Denner & Assocs.

4100 Hudson Home Publications
Designer: Otto Werk

4101

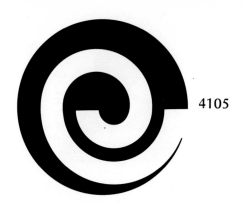
4105

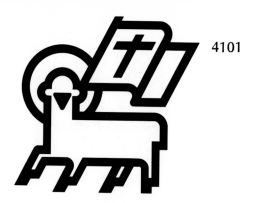
4102

4106

4103

4107

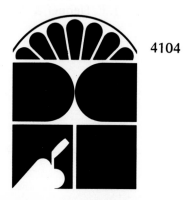
4104

4108

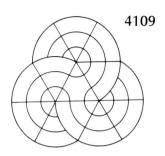

4109

4110

4111

4112

4101 Glen Ridge Congregational Church
Designer: Bill Wood; Design Shop

4102 Friends on the Phone
Designer: Bill Wood; Design Shop

4103 Shalebrook Realty
Designer: Bill Wood; Design Shop

4104 Dymecki Construction Co.
Designer: Bill Wood; Design Shop

4105 Scientific Incineration Devices, Inc.
Designer: Bill Wood; Design Shop

4106 Center for Parish Development
Designer: Bill Wood; Design Shop

4107 Everest Realty
Designer: Bill Wood; Design Shop

4108 Equal Opportunity Employment Service
Designer: Bill Wood; Design Shop

4109 Rogers College
Designer: Bill Wood; Design Shop

4110 Rogers College
Designer: Bill Wood; Design Shop

4111 Cherenson, Carroll & Holzer, Public Relations
Designer: Bill Wood; Design Shop

4112 Channel Companies, Inc.
Designer: Bill Wood; Design Shop

 4113

 4117

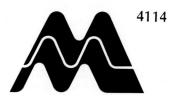 4114

 4118

 4115

 4119

 4116

 4120

4121

4122

4123

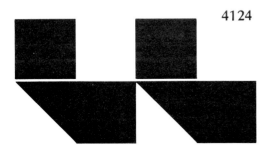

4124

4113 Kings Fairground Mall
      Designer: Bill Wood; Design Shop

4114 MidAtlantic Mortgage Co.
      Designer: Bill Wood; Design Shop

4115 The Design Shop
      Designer: Bill Wood; Design Shop

4116 Glen Ridge Bicentennial Committee
      Designer: Bill Wood; Design Shop

4117 Investors General Estate Corp.
      Designer: Bill Wood; Design Shop

4118 Community Corporation of America
      Designer: Bill Wood; Design Shop

4119 Building and Land Technology Corp.
      Designer: Bill Wood; Design Shop

4120 Acu-Tech Corp.
      Designer: Bill Wood; Design Shop

4121 Educational Data Sciences, Inc.
      Designer: Bill Wood; Design Shop

4122 Brown-Fowler Company Realtors
      Designer: Bill Wood; Design Shop

4123 Green Gallery
      Designer: Bill Wood; Design Shop

4124 L & L Mechanical Contractors, Inc.
      Designer: Roland L. Lee; Ink Well

4125

4129

4126

4130

4127

4131

4128

4132

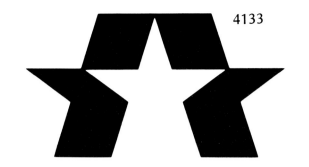

4133

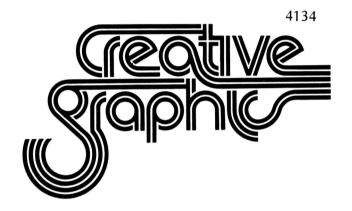

4134

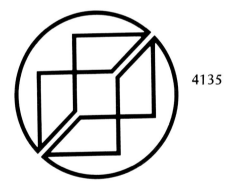

4135

4125 Wes Burke Realty
      Designer: Roland L. Lee; Ink Well

4126 Sunrise Village Townhomes
      Designer: Roland L. Lee; Ink Well

4127 Dixie Ambassadors
      Designer: Roland L. Lee; Ink Well

4128 The Rafters Restaurant
      Designer: Roland L. Lee; Ink Well

4129 Western Food Sales, Inc.
      Designer: Roland L. Lee; Ink Well

4130 Highlands High School, Class of '76
      Designer: Michael Draper

4131 Draper Enterprise Inc.
      Designer: R.A. Draper, Sr.

4132 Robert A. Draper Advertising
      Designer: R.A. Draper Sr./R.A. Draper Jr.

4133 All Stars
      Designer: Mike McMahon

4134 Mike McMahon
      Designer: Mike McMahon

4135 Inside Interiors
      Designer: Mike McMahon

4136 McMahon
      Designer: Mike McMahon

4136

MISSISSIPPI 4137

CAPONE 4138

4139

4141

Robert Powley Photography

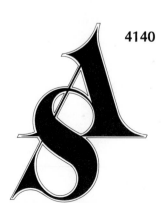

4140

4142

ED GOLDSTEIN PHOTOGRAPHER

4143

4144

4145

4137 McMahon, self-promotion
Designer: Mike McMahon

4138 Capone
Designer: Mike McMahon

4139 Kahuka Sugar Mill
Designer: Bryan Honkawa

4140 Alan Somers Associates
Designer: Bryan Honkawa

4141 Robert Powley
Designer: Bryan Honkawa

4142 Ed Goldstein
Designer: Bryan Honkawa

4143 Petersen Publishing
Designer: Bryan Honkawa

4144 Viking Travel Service
Designer: Schuller, Hawley, Candee Sauerssig

4145 North Dakota Recreation
Designer: Schuller, Hawley, Candee Sauerssig

4146 North Dakota Beef Commission
Designer: Schuller, Hawley, Candee Sauerssig

4146

bismarck parks and
recreation department

4147

4151

4148

MACLD · MINNESOTA ASSOCIATION FOR CHILDREN WITH LEARNING DISABILITIES ·

4152

4149

4153

4150

4154

Thumbnails

4155

4156

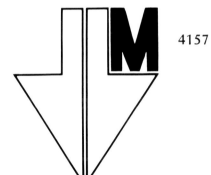

4157

4147 Bismarck Parks & Recreation Dept.
Designer: Schuller, Hawley, Candee Sauerssig

4148 LeFevre Studios Inc.
Designer: LeFevre Studios

4149 Walter H. Leight Co.
Designer: Jurij Kraus; LeFevre Studios

4150 M & R Printing Co., Inc.
Designer: J. Phelpes; LeFevre Studios

4151 Dolph Baumann and Associates
Designer: Eric Madsen

4152 Minnesota Assn. for Children with
        Learning Disabilities
Designer: Eric Madsen

4153 Minnesota Federal Savings & Loan
Designer: Eric Madsen

4154 Thumbnails, Inc.
Designer: Eric Madsen

4155 Fernandez & Rubin
Designer: Eric Madsen

4156 Pine Grove Ranch
Designer: Eric Madsen

4157 Mecca Ventures
Designer: Carole Poole; Charal Assocs.

4158 Atlanta Residential Developers Assn.
Designer: Carole Poole; Charal Assocs.

4158

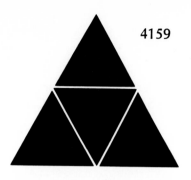

4159

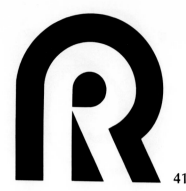

4163

4160

4164

The Orchard Apartments

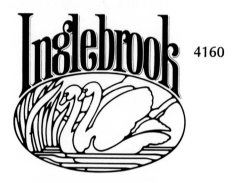

4161

4165

COUNTRY CREEK

4162

TEXAS ART SUPPLY

4166

Systronics

Houston Citizens Bank 4167

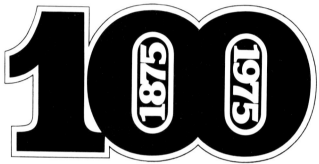

4168

4169

4159 International Systems & Control, Inc.
Designer: Lyle Metzdorf/Rod Lambeth;
Metzdorf Advertising

4160 Ellis Walton Company
Designer: Mark Self; Metzdorf Advertising

4161 Investment Council
Designer: Gayle Ware; Metzdorf Advertising

4162 Texas Art Supply
Designer: Chuck Carlberg
Metzdorf Advertising

4163 Ruhmann Mfg. Co., Inc.
Designer: Rod Lambeth; Metzdorf Advertising

4164 Lincoln Property Management Co.
Designer: Gayle Ware; Metzdorf Advertising

4165 Lincoln Property Management Co.
Designer: Dean Narahara

4166 Systronics
Designer: Rod Lambeth

4167 Houston Citizens Bank
Designer: Herb Lubalin, for Metzdorf Advertising

4168 Houston Citizens Bank
Designer: Herb Lubalin, for Metzdorf Advertising

4169 John Houchins and Sons, Inc.
Designer: Jim Hradecky; Metzdorf Advertising

4170 First National Bank
Designer: Rod Lambeth; Metzdorf Advertising

First National Bank 4170

 4171

 4172

Houston Citizens Bookstore 4173

RAGSDALE, PARDOE' 4174

 4175

4176

4177

4171 Lincoln Property Management Co.
      Designer: Dean Harahara; Metzdorf Advertising

4172 Allen Center
      Designer: Rod Lambeth; Metzdorf Advertising

4173 Houston Citizens Bank
      Designer: Dean Harahara; Metzdorf Advertising

4174 Ragsdale Pardoe
      Designer: Gary Coo; Metzdorf Advertising

4175 Frank Gillman Motorhomes
      Designer: Dean Narahara; Metzdorf Advertising

4176 Blue Bell Creameries
      Designer: Lowell Williams; Metzdorf Advertising

4177 Lincoln Property Management Co.
      Designer: Rod Lambeth; Metzdorf Advertising

ACCELAGARD
4178

4179

7DAV
7 DAY BUILDING SYSTEMS
4180

TSPB
4181

TEXAS SOCIETY FOR THE PREVENTION OF BLINDNESS, INC.

Post Oak Lane
TOWNHOMES
4182

4183

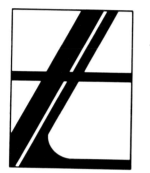

4184

4185

4186

4178 Jeanway Industries
      Designer: Jim Hradecky; Metzdorf Advertising

4179 Lincoln Property Management Co.
      Designer: Dean Narahara; Metzdorf Advertising

4180 Jeanway Industries
      Designer: Jim Hradecky; Metzdorf Advertising

4181 Texas Society for the Prevention of Blindness
      Designer: Jim Hradecky; Metzdorf Advertising

4182 L.B. Nelson Corp. of Texas
      Designer: Lowell Williams; Metzdorf Advertising

4183 The Business Workshop
      Designer: Diane Page/Agostino G. Unti, Jr.;
          Bentley, Barnes & Lynn

4184 Transilwrap Company
      Designer: Agostino G. Unti, Jr.;
          Bentley, Barnes & Lynn

4185 Lauer & Holbrook, Inc.
      Designer: Agostino G. Unti, Jr.;
          Bentley, Barnes & Lynn

4186 Fleeger Trucking
      Designer: Douglas Wilson/Agostino G. Unti, Jr.;
          Bentley, Barnes & Lynn

damson
OIL CORPORATION
4187

meridian
CAPITAL CORPORATION
4188

4189

energine
4190

4191

4192

4187 Damson Oil Corp.
  Designer: Flavian Cresci;
    The Intermar Organization

4188 Meridian Capital Corp. (subsidiary of
    Damson Oil Corp.)
  Designer: Flavian Cresci;
    The Intermar Organization

4189 Playas del Yunque
  Designer: Flavian Cresci;
    The Intermar Organization

4190 Energine
  Designer: Norma Updyke/Jack O'Rourke

4191 Dellwood Dairy
  Designer: Norma Updyke

4192 Kat-trene Products
  Designer: Norma Updyke

4193 Amsterdam Company
  Designer: Norma Updyke

4194 Pulsatron Corporation
  Designer: Norma Updyke/Jack O'Rourke

4193

4194

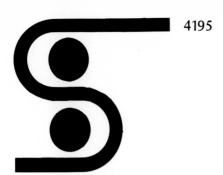 4195

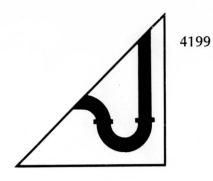 4199

 4196

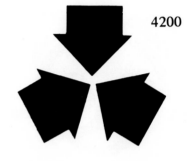 4200

 4197

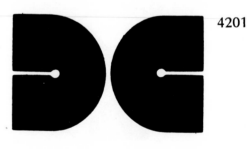 4201

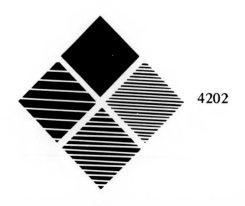 4198

4202

4203

Ashland New Car Dealers Association

4204

4205

RedCom READOUT

4195 Stultz Publishing Co.
Designer: David E. Carter

4196 Ennis Trucking Co.
Designer: David E. Carter

4197 Manley Blade
Designer: David E. Carter

4198 Crooked Mile Farm
Designer: David E. Carter

4199 Johnson Plumbing Co.
Designer: David E. Carter

4200 Tri-State Assn. of Homebuilders
Designer: David E. Carter

4201 Dave Carter Advertising
Designer: David E. Carter

4202 Pollution Control, Inc.
Designer: David E. Carter

4203 Ashland New Car Dealers Assn.
Designer: David E. Carter

4204 General Heating & Air Conditioning
Designer: David E. Carter

4205 US Navy Reserve, Readiness Command
Designer: David E. Carter

Index of Marks

Designers

Addario Design Associates; 176 Newbury Street, Boston, MA 02116

Ainsworth, Ray; Olinkraft, Inc., Post Office Box 488, West Monroe, LA 71291

Anspach, Grossman Inc., 850 Third Avenue, New York, NY 10022

Atvur Associates; 3057 Bolling Way, NE, Atlanta, GA 30305

Avey, Reg; Avey Design, Unit No. 5, 1040 Matley Lane, Reno, NV 89502

Bacigalupi, David, Design; 56 Adler Avenue, San Anselmo, CA 94960

Baker, E.W., Inc.; 55 West Maple Road, Birmingham, MI 48011

Bates, David; 854 West George Street, Chicago, IL 60657

Baxter + Korge, Inc.; 8323 Westglen, Houston, TX 77042

Bentley, Barnes and Lynn, Inc.; 303 East Ohio, Chicago, IL 60611

Benton, Patrick; 3141 Hood Street, Dallas, TX 75219

Bradford-LaRiviera, Saginaw, Michigan

Bradley Yeager & Associates, Inc.; Cobb Building, Post Office Box 9228, Treasure Island, FL 33740

Burlini, Al; Tom Morris, Inc., 621 W. Devon Avenue, Park Ridge, IL 60068

Chapman, William W.; CPS Communications, 2411 W. 8th Street, Los Angeles, CA 90057

Chun, Milton; 4946-4 Kilauea Avenue, Honolulu, Hawaii 96816

Clarke, Chip; 1202 Woodland Avenue, Flatwoods, KY

Company, The; 11340 W. Olympic Blvd., Los Angeles, CA 90064

Corporate Design Systems, Inc.; 210 Commercial Street, Boston, MA 02116

Cottingham, Bruce A.; 2191 Victory Parkway, Cincinnati, OH 45206

Curry, Monte J., Marketing & Communication Services, 921 Baxter Street, Suite 312, Charlotte, NC 28202

Cutler, John G.; 6921 Winterberry Lane, Bethesda, MD 20034

Cutro Associates, 47 Jewett Avenue, Tenafly, NJ 07670

Davis, Don, Design; 212 Edwards Street, Kewanee, IL 61443

Dellinger, Harvey C.; Leslie Advertising Agency, Box 6168, Greenville, SC 29606

Denner, Pat; Suite 801, Ten West Broadway, Salt Lake City, UT 84101

Design Consultants Incorporated; 333 North Michigan Avenue, Chicago, IL 60601

Design-Graphics, Inc.; 450 Tenth Circle N., Nashville, TN 37203

DiCristo, Victor; 741 N. Milwaukee Street, Milwaukee, WI 53202

Directors III, Inc.; 599 New Park Avenue, West Hartford, CT 06110

Drake, Melville M.; The Drake Office, 1409 N. Prospect Avenue, No. 705, Milwaukee, WI 53202

Draper, Robert A., PO Box 69, Ft. Thomas, KY 41075

Dunn, Crawford; RYA Graphics, Inc., Two Lemmon Park East, 3619 Howell Street, Dallas, TX 75204

Emerson/Franzke Advertising, Inc.; Merchants National Building, Topeka, KS 66612

Ensslin Advertising Agency; 102 West Whiting, Tampa, FL 33602

Equitable Graphics, 1285 Avenue of the Americas, New York, NY 10019

Estes, James K.; Roberts Hall, Cornell University, Ithaca, NY 14853

Follis, John and Associates; 2124 Venice Blvd., Los Angeles, CA 90006

Forbes, Everett; 5913 Woodstock Court, Virginia Beach, VA 23462

Franco, Jesus Emilio; Av. Venezuela No. 34, El Rosal, Caracas, 106, Venezuela

Gale, Robert A.; Siegel & Gale; 445 Park Avenue, New York, NY 10022

Gray Whyte Design House; 427 Bloomfield Avenue, Montclair, NJ 07042

Gruel, Jess; Larson/Bateman Inc., 222 E. Anapamo, Santa Barbara, CA 93101

Gutierrez, Frank A.; 2320 Sierra Leone Avenue, Rowland Heights, CA 91748

Gutke, Gordon; 569 Auburn Drive, Murray, UT 84107

Goode, Rex, Organization for Design; 1094 S. Marengo Avenue, Pasadena, CA 91106

Harland, John H., Co.; PO Box 13085, Atlanta, GA 30324

Harper + George Inc.; 18 E. 50 Street, New York, NY 10022

Henton, Tom; Faulkner Watkins & Assocs., 1900 Worthen Bank Building, Little Rock, AR 72201

Herr, Robert; Charles Crone Associates, 417 N. Boylan Avenue, Raleigh, NC 27603

Honkawa, Bryan; Honkawa Design Assocs., 1232 Crescent Heights, Los Angeles, CA 90035

Houston/Ritz/Cohen/Jagoda; 5207 McKinney, Dallas, TX 75205

Huerta Design Associates; 2500 Wilshire Blvd., Los Angeles, CA

Ichiyama, Dennis; Dept. of Design & Environmental Analysis, Cornell University, Ithaca, NY 14850

Ikola, Gale William, and Associates; 6100 Golden Valley Road, Minneapolis, MN 55422

Image Group; 330 Flume Street, Chico, CA 95926

Intermar Organization Ltd., The; 27 East 39 Street, New York, NY 10016

Jacobs, Steven, Designs; Palo Alto, CA

Joseph, Marvin L.; Joseph Advertising Design, 3404 Jefferson, Austin, TX 78703

Kaiser, Mike; Finlay Kaiser & Ballard, Inc.; Suite 999, 924 Westwood Blvd., Los CA 90024

Kannapell, Jack E., Jr.; Cobble Court, Glenview, KY 40025

Kidder Axelson & Associates, Inc.; 10544 West Pico Blvd., Los Angeles, CA 90064

Kiousis, Evan; Gregory, Inc., Cleveland, OH

Klumb, E. Christopher, Associates, Inc.; 333 East 30th Street, New York, NY 10016

Knapp Design Associates; River Forest, IL

Knight, Walsh & Associates, Inc.; 3202 E. 21 Street, Tulsa, OK 74114

Krackehl, Gene; 5-36 117th Street, College Point, NY 11356

Krispinsky, L.S.; Second Dimension Studio, 4405 Aspen Drive, Youngstown, OH 44515

LaBahn, Arnold; Peoples Gas Co., 122 S. Michigan Avenue, Chicago, IL 60603

Lake Advertising Art; 210 St. Paul, Denver, CO 80206

Landor, Walter, Associates; Ferryboat Klamath, Pier 5, San Francisco, CA 94111

Lane & Leslie Advertising Agency, Inc.; PO Box 978, Hutchinson, KS 67501

Lee, Roland L.; Ink Well, 101 N. Main, No. 3, St. George, UT 84770

LeFevre Studios, Inc.; 550 Main Street East, Rochester, NY 14604

Leigh, David; 1245 Park Avenue, New York, NY 10028

Leitstein, Alan Stuart; 8360 NW 21 Ct., Sunrise, FL 33313

Leslie Advertising Agency; Box 6168, Greenville, SC 29606

Lindsay, Dean R.; Center for Advanced Research in Design; 645 N. Michigan Ave., Chicago, IL 60611

Lippincott & Margulies; 277 Park Avenue, New York, NY 10017

Lipson-Jacobs & Associates; 2349 Victory Parkway, Cincinnati, OH 45206

Litten, Reginald K.; Sugarcreek Concepts, 221 Greenmount Blvd., Dayton, OH 45419

Lubliner/Saltz; 509 Madison Avenue, New York, NY 10020

Maccaroni, James N.; Parker Allen Co., 1309 Highland Avenue, Abington, PA 19001

Madsen, Eric; Thumbnails, Inc.; 505 E. Grant St., Minneapolis, MN 55404

Maish, Jay H., Company; 280 N. Main Street, Marion, OH 43302

Manning, Robert C., George & Glover Advertising Agency, 712 W. Peachtree, Atlanta, GA 30308

Martel, Marie; 1311 East Edgemont, Phoenix AZ 85006

Martin-Remick-Moore Advertising; PO Box 7328, 1004 N. Thompson Street, Richmond, VA 23221

McMahon, Mike; 170 Holland Drive, Virginia Beach, VA 23462

Metzdorf Advertising Agency, Inc.; 1929 Allen Parkway, 5th Floor, Houston, TX 77019

Miller, Mike; Graphic Art Services. 2141 Industrial Road, Las Vegas, NV 89102

Mock, Mark; 5030 Quitman Street, Denver, CO 80212

Morgado, Richard, Designer; 179 Jerrold Street, Holliston, MA 01746

Murphy, David M.; David Manufacturing Co., 1600 12th Street, NE, Mason City, IA 50401

Oei Enterprises Ltd.; 620 Pelham Road, New Rochelle, NY 10805

Overlock Howe & Company; 915 Olive Street, St. Louis, MO 63101

Pacey, Michael; Supergraphics, 603-990 Broughton Street, Bancouver, BC, Canada

Partain, Daniel M.; 1801 Avenue of the Stars, Suite 1000, Los Angeles, CA 90067

Paul, Rolf H., Graphics; 171 Red Rocks Vista Lane, Box 48, Morrison, CO 80465

Pelini, Lawrence E., Studio; 213 S. Jefferson Peoria, IL 61602

Penniman, Edward G., and Associates; 1537½ Pacific Avenue, Santa Cruz, CA 95060

Phillips, Wyatt L.; Marketing Advisory Group, 1354 West Wesley Road, NW, Atlanta, GA 30327

Pieslak, Jon, 224 Clarendon Street, Boston, MA 02116

Point Communications, Inc.; Post Oak Tower, Suite 415, 5051 Westheimer, Houston, TX 77027

Poole, Carole; Charal Associates, Inc. 5600 Roswell Road, Suite 280, Atlanta, GA 30342

Potocki, James L.; Huerta Design Associates, 2500 Wilshire Blvd., Los Angeles, CA

Primi, Don; Industrial Advertising Associates Inc., Station Plaza East, Great Neck, NY 11021

Purdon, Jac; 16934 Village Lane, Grosse Pointe, MI 48230

Quon, Mike; 1516 Westwood Blvd., 104, Los Angeles, CA 90024

Rabe, Peter J.; 2650 W. Mock Orange Dr., Salt Lake City, UT 84119

Rainey, David, Graphic Design; 600 Stemmons Tower South, Dallas, TX 75207

Reeves, Dyke & Co.; PO Box 27359, Houston, TX 77027

Reynolds, Stephen; 120 Brunswick Street, Rochester, NY 14607

Richards Group, The; Fidelity Union Tower, Dallas, TX 75201

Ritta, Kay; Ritta Design, 197 Sherwood Place, Englewood, NJ 07631

Robinson, George; 572 Kings Road, Yardley PA 19067

Roth, Randall R.; 535 N. Michigan Avenue, Chicago, IL 60611

Ruedy, Jeanie; 402 Oil & Gas Building, Oklahoma City, OK 73102

Sandgren & Murtha, Inc.; 866 Third Avenue, New York, NY

Sandhaus, Paul, Associates; 99 Park Avenue, New York, NY 10016

Saunders, Edward A.; 1314 Victoria Street, No. 203, Honolulu, HI 96814

Schecter and Luth; 430 Park Avenue, New York, NY 10022

Schlosser, Cyril John; 4317 York Avenue South, Minneapolis, MN 55410

Schuller, Hawley, Candee, Sauerssig Adv., Inc.; PO Box 693, Bismarck, ND 58501

Seifert, William; 350 E. 52 Street, Apt. 12-K, New York, NY 10022

Selje, Bond & Stewart; 1414 Fair Oaks Avenue, So. Pasadena, CA 91030

Sepetys, George N. and Associates, Inc.; 26111 Evergreen, Suite 320, Southfield, MI 48075

Skaggs, Steve, 546 Ridgecrest Road, NE, Atlanta, GA 30307

Smith, F. Eugene, Associates; Bath, OH

Soos, Anita, Design; 420 B Highland Ave., Cheshire, CT 06410

Spivey, Wm, Design; 3740 Campus Drive, Suite C, Newport Beach, CA 92660

Starr, E. Clark; Wells Drive, Farmington, CT 06032

Sterrenburg, Don; 8 Essex Place, Chalmsford, MA 01824

Steward, Tom; 400 Thurber Dr., W, No. 12, Columbus, OH 43215

Suggs, J. David; 1420 Lady Street, Columbia, SC 29201

Sychowski, Robert; People's Gas Co., 122 S. Michigan Avenue, Chicago, IL 60603

Sykes, David; Department of Communication Arts, Cornell University, Ithaca, NY 14850

Taylor, Pat, Inc.; 3540 "S" Street, NW, Washington, DC 20007

Thomas, Charles; Thomas Design, 822 Olive, Chico, CA 95926

Tolman, Kevin; Artra Associates, 26555 Evergreen, Southfield, MI 48076

Triad Associates; PO Box 1305, Waco, TX 76703

Tscherny, George, Inc.; 238 E. 72 Street, New York, NY 10021

Turzio, Paul; 236 Evergreen Avenue, Staten Island, NY 10305

Unti, Agostino G.; Bentley, Barnes & Lynn, 303 East Ohio, Chicago, IL 60611

Updyke, Norma E.; River Glen, Studio 26, Hastings-on-Hudson, NY 10706

Vanderbyl, Michael, Graphic Design; 1000 Sansome Street, San Francisco, CA 94111

Visual Design Center, Inc.; 108 N. State St., Chicago, IL 60602

Walker, James M.; Walker, Knudson & Campbell, Inc., 545 Rue Royale, Covina, CA 91723

Weiser, Paul S.; Kilbourn Studios, 1501 Monroe Avenue, Rochester, NY 14618

Weller, Don; The Weller Institute for the Cure of Design, 340 Mavis Drive, Los Angeles, CA 90065

Werk, Otto; Studio Werk, Inc., 200 California Avenue, Palo Alto, CA 94306

Weston, Al; 3476 Newgate Road, Troy, MI 48084

Wickliffe, Barry; Jennings & Thompson Advertising, Inc., 2200 North Central Avenue, Phoenix, AZ 85004

Wideroe, Bernard M.; Primary Design, 1816 Wells, Chicago, IL 60614

Woo, Calvin; Humangraphic, 3776 Front Street, San Diego, CA 92103

Wood, Bill; The Design Shop, 68 Winsor Place, Glen Ridge, NJ 07028

Zimmermann, Mel; Mel Zimmermann & Associates, 317 N. 11th Street, St. Louis, MO 63101